LOOKING *for the* NATION

Towards Another Idea of India

Manash Firaq Bhattacharjee

SPEAKING TIGER PUBLISHING PVT. LTD
4381/4, Ansari Road, Daryaganj
New Delhi 110002

Published in India by Speaking Tiger in paperback 2018

Copyright © Manash Bhattacharjee 2018

ISBN: 978-93-88070-41-6
eISBN: 978-93-88070-02-7

10 9 8 7 6 5 4 3 2 1

Typeset in Sabon Roman by SŪRYA, New Delhi
Printed at Sanat Printers, Kundli

All rights reserved.
No part of this publication may be reproduced, transmitted,
or stored in a retrieval system, in any form or by any
means, electronic, mechanical, photocopying,
recording or otherwise, without the prior
permission of the publisher.

This book is sold subject to the condition that it shall not, by
way of trade or otherwise, be lent, resold, hired out, or otherwise
circulated, without the publisher's prior consent,
in any form of binding or cover other than
that in which it is published.

To

Zafar Aqueel,
whose Eid wasn't complete without Kishore Kumar

Bidhan S. Laishram,
for remaining a Meitei among Indians

Abir Bazaz,
for speaking the Kashmir of his schizophrenia

Contents

Preface: The Manipulation of History	ix
1. The Surplus of Indian Nationalism	1
2. Territory without Justice	62
3. Looking for the Muslim	79
4. The Nation's Untouchables	104
5. The Nation's Bodies	123
6. Thinking Against Power	150
Postscript: On the Future of Politics	167
Acknowledgements	183
Bibliography	185
Index	197

Preface

The Manipulation of History

> (W)e need not go to the past to find instances of the manipulation of history to suit particular ends and support one's own fancies and prejudices...
>
> —Jawaharlal Nehru,
> *The Discovery of India*

While growing up in a small town in Assam, a friend of my father, a retired railway employee, would often visit our house. The old man would occasionally break into stories, telling my elder sister and me about the violence of Partition. These stories inevitably revolved around Muslims attacking Hindu villages and towns, and innovative strategies evolved by Hindus to ward off the attacks. I remember one particular incident he narrated, where scores of bricks were stored on the terraces of Hindu households in a particular locality in East Bengal. When the Muslims attacked, the bricks were put to effective use. We never wondered why he chose to tell a fourteen-year-old boy and his sister stories that would shake them to the bone. It took me many years to realize not only the deliberate pattern of the stories, but also the intention behind his telling them. The man, I learnt much later, belonged to a Hindu right-wing organization. The stories he told us were a part of his job. His job was propaganda. This was a politically sanctioned method to arouse and cement communal sentiments.

The old man's efforts did not work. I was unimpressed by the rousing talk of elderly Bengali men. Their language of cultural pride never swayed me. It probably had to do with their general tone and mannerisms about everything; I did not take to their commanding ways very well. I was bad with rules, be it in school, at home, or anywhere else. I thought, like Albert Camus, that the very essence of being a human being was to reject rules and commands.

I also had a Muslim friend in school. Friendship mattered more to me than family and religion. Friendship is the first occasion where your heart discovers its affinity for a stranger, and the feeling is liberating. You don't need a book or a sermon to teach you something life does. Life does not lie to you, unlike the people you may meet in life. Lying was the old man's political job. Once he narrated a conversation between Atal Bihari Vajpayee and George W. Bush on the Hindu-Muslim question in India, vis-à-vis the race question in America. He narrated the story in an intimate style, making us feel he was present when the conversation took place. I later learnt from a well-read neighbour that this conversation was an imaginary one, part of the propaganda. Telling such lies was the man's habit. But the poor man wasn't as convincing to a fourteen-year-old as he thought. It was perhaps some sort of miracle that I listened to his stories without falling for their logic.

Hate is logical. So is fear. Those who spread stories to arouse hate know the old law of a community, where the mysterious quality of human blood is prone to err against the stranger, or the outsider. It is called the law of preservation and has a biological ring to it. But the human spirit is also prone to love. It changes the direction of blood. Love breaks the law of preservation by *risking*.

In his commentary on G.W.F. Hegel's *Phenomenology of Spirit*, Russian-born French philosopher and statesman,

Alexandre Kojève, explains Hegel's argument: 'For man to be truly human...his human Desire must actually win out over his animal Desire...All the Desires of an animal are in the final analysis a function of its desire to preserve its life. Human Desire, therefore, must win out over this Desire for preservation. In other words, man's humanity "comes to light" only if he *risks* his (animal) life for the sake of his human Desire' (Emphasis added). Hegel seeks to differentiate between two kinds of desire: one, that keeps us bound to the self-preservation of life, akin to the animal spirit. The other desire pushes us to extend our limits and embrace or risk the unfamiliar, akin to the human spirit.

Here, I would contest Hegel's idea of risk—which contributes to being human—as *only* a desire for power. Such risk is merely the desire for violence and a self-preserving authority. It is no different from animal desire. If power alone introduces risk into history through its logic of violence, it is a calculable risk, for power works within a calculable desire for self-preservation. Risk without (or against) power is *incalculable*. The slave, by seeking freedom, risks not power or slavery, but death.

The desire for (animal) self-preservation is intrinsically related to the idea of territoriality. Hegel's master-slave dialectic works within the logic of territory, which remains unaltered by either risk or labour. Doesn't the human condition too become an extension of the animal, in its territorializing idea of life? Doesn't colonialism, a territorial mission, introduce the desire for a territorially sacrosanct nation? In the name of 'human civilization', the civilizing mission of the West spread its racist tentacles through Asia and Africa. The West invented the nation as a new idea (and law) of territory, circumscribing the idea of the human. It was a new law of self-preservation. Both Hegel and Kojève are equally guilty of enthusiasm for this new, territorial 'humanity'.

A nation, instead of encouraging risk, tries to prevent and eliminate it, in order to preserve itself. Tagore understood this malady, as he wrote in his essay 'Nationalism in the West' with brilliant precision: 'the Nation is the greatest evil for the Nation...all its precautions are against it.' The nation is narcissistic and can love only itself. Only by desiring the stranger, the other, by undoing the law of territory and the self-preserving logic of animalistic life, can our existence 'come to light,' as Kojève said. This undoing has to include Hegelian ideals of nation and state (as well as Kojève's), and look for values *other* than the ideas of universality and 'humanity'.

In *We or Our Nationhood Defined*, M.S. Golwalkar uses the terms 'hereditary territory' and race (defined internally as 'hereditary society') as two fundamental aspects of the nation. He treats modern Germany as the perfect example for his definition of a nation. Fascism is a strict, logical equation. Race=territory=nation. B.R. Ambedkar, in *The Untouchables: Who Were They and Why They Became Untouchables*, uses the term 'hereditary untouchability' to define the logic of the Hindu caste system and the practice of untouchability. The law of heredity goes against the idea of equality. The idea of democracy, built on the rule of law, or equality before law, is opposed to the idea of heredity.

A 'hereditary society' justifies inequality. It is against the idea of equality, dignity and freedom. When incorporated in the idea of a nation, the combination of race and hereditary society marks its territory to exclude people and enforce the sentiment of self-preservation on those it includes. Such an idea of the nation works against the desire to be what Kojève called 'truly human'.

Indian nationalist thinkers were most unique in their refutations. Nehru's refutation of religious nationalism of any kind (including the Gandhian) was firm and sincere. His quest to 'discover' India, despite its borrowing of the dominant modes of Western thought, made an attempt to create an affirmative Orientalism challenging British rule. Gandhi's refutation of Western modernity (though partly rhetorical) was a radical gesture. His idea of nonviolence put the history of the modern West to shame. Tagore's refutation of nationalism is without parallel, posed remarkably outside all dominant schools of twentieth-century political thought. Aurobindo made a unique refutation of the idea of the 'sacred' as a basis for a spiritual nation. Ambedkar's refutation of Hindu society as one where morality is possible, offers a radical critique of the caste system and untouchability.

Hindu nationalism is antithetical to the ideas of all these thinkers. Taking its founding principles from Golwalkar's ideas, it is a pathologically sentimental idea that exploits the communal pangs of Partition in arguing for a nation where segregation and hierarchy are justified. The Hindu nationalist takeover of India's polity has been accompanied by terrible violence against Dalits and Muslims. Instead of timely condemnation, state officials end up encouraging religious vigilantism, be it in the name of cow protection or 'love jihad'. The unfolding crisis in India's postcolonial history urges a *political* need to critically revisit the bold, open and humane ideas that marked the beginning of this nation. To return to those ideas is also to return to old wounds, follies and contestations. The degeneration of secular politics has no place to hide its face either. The politics of risk which enabled the promising mass movements of anticolonial nationalism, has been replaced by the politics of self-preservation. It is being legitimized today in the name of national security. Meanwhile, there is a concerted move to communalize our history.

If communism manipulates history in the name of a classless society to come, and if secular-democratic politics allows only a rationalist order of nationalist discourses to prosper, fascism of all varieties manipulates history to reinstate the origin of prejudice.

At this difficult juncture of our history, the memory of my father's friend came to mind. His lies and fantasies have caught up with my present. This is my act of resistance against his ghost. In this book, I am not looking for a desirable idea of the nation. I am looking for the nation with irony, discovering everything that falls short of fraternity and justice. I am looking at another possibility, *another* idea of an India, where nationalism is a matter of disinterest. People, particularly those who are less privileged and fewer in number, matter more than nations. Nationalism is the celebration of power. The idea of justice, like the idea of ethics, is *bent* towards the vulnerable other. Looking for the nation, I look at possibilities of a new fraternity. Perhaps that will usher in a new politics of trust.

1

The Surplus of Indian Nationalism

Indian nationalist thought is a product of the anticolonial movement. Thinkers, who took part in the nationalist struggle against British colonialism, also wrote extensively, sometimes in print, and often in response to each other's ideas. Nehru lays down the larger debate of nationalism, and its relation with modernity, culture, identity and history. Aurobindo reflects on the nation as a grand idea in the shadow of religious differences. Tagore engages with Gandhi on the question of culture and argues for universalism. Gandhi's new political ethic based on nonviolence and trust offers a cultural critique of colonial modernity. Ambedkar opens up the debate on caste by historicizing it. It exposes the political limits of Indian nationalism. The 'surplus' of Indian nationalism involves speculations by nationalist thinkers around the question of (spiritual) culture. Ambedkar provides a critical perspective.

~

Almost forty years before Benedict Anderson gave us the description of the nation as 'an imagined political community,' Jawaharlal Nehru had constructed a nationalist history through which he wanted to 'discover' India. This attempt to discover the nation broadly meant two kinds of questions for Nehru. The first was: 'What is this India? What did she represent in the past?...How does she fit into the modern world?' The idea of India appeared to be ready for more content, waiting for Nehru to give it a shape and dress it up for modernity. Thus Nehru marked himself as a suitable tailor of the nationalist discourse. His other question was, 'Did I know India?' Here, he is seized by the predicament peculiar to the modern subject, where (lacking) knowledge about the nation is part of self-anxiety.

As Stuart Hall pointed out, the notion of 'the West' is 'an idea, a concept'. Nehru's conception of 'India' also emerges as a representation that seeks independent classification. The voyages by Europeans led to their conquest of other lands and its domination of the globe. It resulted in the racist and Orientalist discourse, where Christopher Columbus 'discovered' America and Vasco da Gama 'discovered' India. All that Columbus accidentally discovered, in 1492, was a sea route across the Pacific. The discovery violently interrupted the life of other peoples, America's natives, as Columbus did not hesitate to indulge in trans-atlantic slave trade and the genocide of Hispaniola's natives. The Cape of Good Hope was good to da Gama, who followed the clues left by Bartolomeu Dias ten years earlier and found a trade route to India in 1497, bypassing the Muslim territories of the Mediterranean Sea and the Arabian Peninsula. This eventually led to British colonialism.

Nehru's attempt at discovering his own nation a few centuries later is, in contrast, an inward voyage, analogous to cultural self-discovery. It is marked by resistance and hesitation to discover something historically tainted by power, a land that is both real and an idea. The meaning of Nehru's 'discovery' is a marked departure from the borrowed generality of the 'Orient'. It is a speculative attempt to try to address, in some measure, what Benedict Anderson calls the 'philosophical poverty' of nationalism.

Delivering the Azad Memorial Lectures in 1959, Nehru spoke about the paradoxical nature of the historical moment where 'we stand facing both ways, forward the future and backwards the past, being pulled in two directions'. Time was a predicament, for the advent of colonial modernity had split time into past and present, old and new. How did Nehru understand the relationship with the past and determine his choice for the future? In *The Discovery of India*, written between 1942 and 1946 at the Ahmednagar fort prison where he was confined for participating in the Quit India Movement, Nehru writes:

> 'Some Hindus talk of going back to the Vedas; some Moslems dream of an Islamic theocracy. Idle fancies, for there is no going back to the past; there is no turning back even if this was thought desirable. There is only one-way traffic in Time.'

Nehru echoes a definitive bias for the linear idea (and time) of progress. The problem does not lie in Nehru's endorsement of the values of criticism and social change that define the Enlightenment spirit of the modern era. What is troubling is to read his confidence in the modern world which is driven by the self-assurance that a critique of the past secures it from its follies, and inevitably leads to progress. There is a hole in its justificatory logic that (the use of) reason is liberation. This positivist idea of knowledge that (scientific, verifiable) reason alone can best interpret and determine the truth about human beings and their experiences, raises more questions than answers.

Nehru has clear ideas about what entails progress in the social sphere (along with certain misgivings). He wanted India to 'lessen her religiosity and turn to science.' He equates religiosity with 'social habit', complaining that the 'idea of ceremonial purity has erected barriers against social intercourse and narrowed the sphere of social action.' This brings us to

Nehru's naming of the social habit which he thinks has no place in modernity:

> Caste has in the past not only led to the suppression of certain groups, but to a separation of theoretical and scholastic learning from craftsmanship...This outlook has to change completely, for it is wholly opposed to modern conditions and the democratic ideal.

Nehru acknowledges caste as a unique form of social exploitation, where division of labour is ascertained by birth. But Nehru locates the problem of caste in people's 'outlook', which is liberal superficiality. He ignores the deeper, structural origins of casteism in scripture, practice, and in what Ambedkar called 'notion'. For that matter, one wonders why Nehru, in *The Discovery* (and even later), which he began to write six years after the publication of Ambedkar's *The Annihilation of Caste* (and Gandhi's response in *Harijan* on 11 July 1936), never mentions or engages with Ambedkar's unprecedented attack on the caste system.

Nehru's next demand was to widen the democratic principle:

> In India, at any rate, we must aim at equality. That does not and cannot mean that everybody is physically or intellectually or spiritually equal or can be made so. But it does mean equal opportunities for all and no political, economic, or social barrier in the way of any individual or group.

Nehru acknowledges that individuals are incommensurable beings. But equality alone ensures the free flowering of individuality. He then attaches this social ideal with an economic one:

> If the spirit of the age demands equality, it must necessarily also demand an economic system which fits in with it and encourages it. That change will have to be in the direction of a

democratically planned collectivism. A democratic collectivism need not mean an abolition of private property, but it will mean the public ownership of the basic and major industries. It will mean the co-operative or collective control of the land.

Even though Nehru's social ideal is based on liberal individualism, he borrows his economic idea, if only in part, from Marxism-Leninism. Democratic collectivism, apart from Nehru's description, also addresses inequality of wealth through proportionate taxation. Partha Chatterjee makes a critical note of how Nehru's 'appropriation of Marxism was...deliberately selective', as he chose to 'embrace the rationalist and egalitarian side of Marxism, leaving its political core well alone.'

Sanjay Seth responded to this criticism, pointing out that even as 'Nehru's thought was consistent and coherent in its use of Marxism', it also *equally consistently and coherently* yielded a non-Marxist politics'. Seth argued: 'In the colonies, where Marxism was not a critique of modernity, and where it was shorn of a distinctive political core, it could be appropriated by a rationalist and modernizing nationalism without doing violence to Marxism'. Violence to Marxism is a matter of ideological purity and not an ethical concern. Any justificatory form of 'rationalist and modernizing nationalism' is prone to commit implicit violence (for example, Marxists ignored the question of caste in India and subsumed it under their favoured category of class), or explicit violence (for example, the 1979 state-sponsored genocide by the Left Front Government in West Bengal, of the 'Namashudras'—Bengali Dalit refugees from Bangladesh who lived on an island called Marichjhhapi in the Sundarbans).

Nehru corroborates Seth's point in the Azad Memorial Lectures, by specifying the understanding behind his non-Marxist politics: 'Marx was primarily moved by the ghastly conditions that prevailed in the early days of industrialization in Western Europe. At that time there was no truly democratic structure of the state, and changes could hardly be made constitutionally. Hence, revolutionary violence offered the only way to change. Marxism therefore, inevitably thought in terms of a violent revolution. Since then, however, political democracy has spread bringing with it the possibility of peaceful change...' Nehru's interest in Marxism falls within his commitment to democracy, and is limited by it.

It is Nehru's critical understanding of European history that perhaps prevented him from such ideological fixity. The Mexican poet-critic Octavio Paz, in his memorial lecture on Nehru in Delhi in 1967, makes the observation that Nehru's 'relations with Europe were critical and this criticism was based on the heterodox tradition of the West itself.' Paz goes on to fiercely extol Nehru against his authoritarian contemporaries in the world: 'In contrast to the majority of the political leaders of this century, Nehru did not believe that he held the keys of history in his hands. Because of this, he did not stain his country nor the world with blood.' In *The Discovery*, Nehru does air his doubts about his belief in linear time and the accompanying ideology of positivism: 'Or again, perhaps, the very progress of science, unconnected with and isolated from moral discipline and ethical considerations, will lead to the concentration of power.' This awareness leads Nehru in the Azad Memorial Lectures: 'Communists have become the metaphysicians of the present age.'

In *The Discovery*, Nehru made a severe indictment of Indian communists, writing: 'I know that in India the Communist Party is completely divorced from, and is ignorant of, the national traditions that fill the minds of the people. It believes that communism necessarily implies a contempt for the past.' Nehru tried to escape the positivist bias which influenced him quite strongly as well, by conceding a more paradoxical approach to the idea of progress: 'National progress can... neither lie in a repetition of the past nor in its denial.' He puts forward an idea of the present as a critical variation of the past wherein progress is to be measured by its evaluative aspect. The responsibility expected of modern minds is to think the present by retrieving all that is valuable from the past.

Paz was right in asserting that—'Nehru's faith in science and technology was not absolute...He knew that contradiction is not an accident but a law: the very substance of history and man himself.' Despite his optimism for the idea of progress in modernity, Nehru reflected on its limitations in *The Discovery*: 'There is something lacking in all this progress, which can neither produce harmony between nations nor within the spirit of man. Perhaps more synthesis and a little humility towards the wisdom of the past...would help us to gain a new perspective and greater harmony.'

What is the 'spirit of man' which Nehru refers to? It appears to be a vague, speculative idea of something that can feel and measure what modernity lacks. It also refers to an excess, or surplus, a spirit that exceeds the materialist conditions of modernity. We shall see Tagore introduce the idea (and category) of 'surplus' also in terms of the human 'spirit'.

Soon after he acknowledges—echoing a Gandhian sensibility—that modern civilization 'has something counterfeit about it', Nehru contextualizes the 'spirit of man' in this defining paragraph:

> What is wrong with modern civilization which produces...signs of sterility and racial decadence?...Modern industrialism and the capitalist structure of society cannot be the sole causes, for decadence has often occurred without them...If the basic cause is something spiritual, something affecting the mind and spirit of man, it is difficult to grasp though we may try to understand it or intuitively feel it.

The 'spirit of man' is clearly a cultural/spiritual entity in contradistinction with the materialism of western modernity which became a part of the colonies. The 'spirit of man', as a cultural surplus, exceeds the visible signs of material existence and enables us to speculate on its limitations.

Nehru contrasts 'the spirit of the age' as 'represented by the west' with 'the deeper lessons of life, which have absorbed the minds of thinkers in all ages and in all countries'. He does not emphasize an idea of cultural exclusivity. Nehru's idea is explicitly universal and implicitly heterogeneous. To reiterate this point, he says elsewhere in *The Discovery*, 'But there is a special heritage for those of us in India, not an exclusive one, for none is exclusive and all are common to the race of man.' Nehru does not pose cultural specificity in relativistic terms. In fact, he does not adhere to the idea of any 'fundamental difference between the Orient and the Occident'. There is however a difference that Nehru marks in economic terms: 'I do not understand the use of the words Orient and Occident, except in the sense that Europe and America are highly industrialized and Asia is backward in this respect.' In Nehru's 'rebuttal of the essentialist dichotomy between Eastern and Western cultures', Partha Chatterjee finds (Indian) 'nationalist thought has come to grips with the Orientalist thematic.'

Nehru does not hold on to the spiritual/material dichotomy in the straightforward manner in which it appeared in post-Enlightenment rationalist (and positivist) thought in Europe. He writes in *The Discovery*: 'The bitter conflict between science and religion which shook up Europe in the nineteenth century would have no reality in India, nor would change based on the applications of science bring any conflict with those ideals.'

In *The Discovery*, Nehru writes:

> The impact of western culture on India was the impact of a dynamic society, a 'modern' consciousness, on a static

society wedded to medieval habits of thought which, however sophisticated and advanced in their own way, could not progress because of its inherent limitations. And, yet, curiously enough, the agents of this historic process were not only wholly unconscious of their mission in India, but, as a class, actually represented no such process...In India they had a free field and were successful in applying the brakes to that very change and progress which, in the larger context, they represented...If change came it was in spite of them.

Paz, in his 1967 lecture, noted how, in the context of British colonialism in India, Nehru 'saw the opposition between East and West as the clash between two historical realities'. Paz observes that 'for Nehru, the clash between different cultures was rather fictitious; the real thing was the historical opposition'. So we find yet another distinction made by Nehru—between culture and history. He raises the question of identity, which is modern, but does not come from the premises of Enlightenment rationality alone. It also comes from a romantic sense of individuality where a person belongs both inside and outside of one's culture. It comes from a lived experience of cultural heterogeneity which is not simply a matter of critical engagement with one's tradition. Paz concludes that, 'Contrary to the anthropologists and the historians who postulate the multiplicity of cultures, Nehru affirmed the unity of thought and the universality of science, art and technology. In this universality, he saw the answer to the antagonism of the historical worlds'. Considering Paz's assessment, the promise of universality premised upon scientific thought and rationality finds an unreflective adherent in Nehru. Universality is part of the ideological baggage of Western modernity, and aids the hegemonic project of colonialism. Universality created new antagonisms by inferiorizing cultural specificities and practices in purely rational terms. This problem escaped Nehru's alert mind.

For Nehru, colonialism was an exploitative ideology of power produced by the expansionist zeal of a narrow-minded class of Englishmen who were themselves against the essence of modernity—whose values should ideally make it impossible for one culture to exploit another. Colonialism betrayed the very baggage of modernity it brought to India's doorstep. The colonialist presented the dichotomy as part of their grand narrative of colonialism. Nehru's observation is analytical and critical. It counters the colonial narrative by positing liberation against domination. It raises a crucial question, that whether representation of say, backwardness, can justify domination. The relationship between representation and domination includes the question of intentionality and agency. In Nehru's case, the thematic of the intentional object, the Indian 'nation', is represented in a critical and evolutionary manner, dissolving the Orientalist dichotomy between the East and the West in ethnocentric (and essentialist) terms. Intentionality grants autonomy to thinking, despite the imbalance of power in the interaction between Western knowledge and Indian predicaments. The question of autonomy can't be posed 'outside' the interaction between the West and India. This view challenges Partha Chatterjee's contention that the Indian nationalist discourse is 'inauthentic' because of its 'lack of autonomy'. Autonomy is always the autonomy to choose. The choice of values that constitute an ethical difference between cultures, exceeds arguments based on mere ethnocentrism. As an ethical idea, the promise of universalism is best secured in gestures that question power, rather than norms that reaffirm it. Between ethnocentrism and an *a priori* notion of universalism lies, what Michel Walzer calls 'reiterative universalism'.

Nehru wrote in his *Autobiography* about being 'accused by some leaders of the Hindu Mahasabha' of his 'ignorance of Hindu sentiments' because of his 'defective education and general background of "Persian" culture'. Nehru responded to this accusation with honest reluctance and vagueness: 'What culture I possess, or whether I possess any at all, is a little difficult for me to say.' By his own admission, though India was in Nehru's 'blood', he 'approached her like an alien critic', and '[t]o *some* extent...came to her via the West' (Emphasis added). This unique predicament of a modernist subject, who is part insider and part outsider, undergoes a *partial* sense of apology. It is also inflicted by the so-called 'culturally rooted' people who force 'outsiders', in the words of Zygmunt Bauman, 'to prove the legality of their presence'. The demand for such legality points to the uneasy relationship between culture and history.

Paz, in his 1967 lecture, described Nehru as one who 'belonged to a double anti-tradition'. Educated at Harrow and Cambridge, Nehru developed close links with European culture and, as Paz points out, 'drew inspiration from the rebellious and heterodox thought of the West'. Nehru's other lineage is traced by Paz back to his ancestors who 'had frequented the Mogul court and had absorbed Persian and Arabic heritage', and to his family tradition from which 'he had a vein of heterodoxy vis-à-vis Hindu traditionalism'. It is a combination of the anxiety of being an 'alien critic', along with this necessity of producing a narrative of the nation, which makes Nehru think about the task of the historian. *The Discovery* eloquently suffered from all the signs Homi Bhabha pointed to in his enumeration of the pitfalls of nationalist reconstruction.

In his introduction to *Narrating the Nation*, Bhabha writes of the 'impossibly romantic and excessively metaphorical' image of the nation. This is exactly what Nehru creates in this gendered evocation of India: 'Shameful and repellent she is occasionally, perverse and obstinate, sometimes even a little hysteric, this lady with a past.' Bhabha also writes how 'nations, like narratives, lose their origins in the myths of time and only fully realize their horizons in the mind's eye.' It suggests the mentalist source of nationalist imagination, although, when Nehru finds India 'a myth and an idea, a dream and a vision', he suggests the possibility of non-mentalist sources of reception as well. In contrast to Salman Rushdie's Pakistan in *Shame*, which is 'failure of the dreaming mind...just insufficiently imagined', Nehru's India is over-imagined, its history spilling over into myth, blurring the lines. No nation can be dreamt enough, for all territories are rationally bound and determined.

~

In *The Discovery*, Nehru felt reason should play second fiddle to the issue of Partition and the relation between Hindu and Muslim communities: 'It is clear that any real settlement must be based on the goodwill of the constituent elements and on the desire of all parties to it to cooperate together for a common objective. In order to gain that *any sacrifice in reason* is worthwhile. Every group must not only be theoretically and actually free and have equal opportunities of growth, but should have the sensation of freedom and equality' (Emphasis added). Confronted by the Hindu-Muslim question, Nehru emphasizes the affective quality of 'goodwill', rather than political rationality. In fact, he is unusually emphatic about abandoning reason if it served to bridge community sentiments. Nehru sounds closer to Gandhi's quest for mutual trust between communities as the prime motivation towards solving political disputes. He of course includes the universalist principles of freedom and equality as the basis (or precondition) for negotiating political claims.

And yet, when Nehru later summed up the Congress attitude to Partition, he sounded quite different: 'The Congress was prepared to do anything within the *bounds of reason* to remove fear and suspicion from the mind of any Province or community, but it felt itself unable to endorse [any suggestion that] went against the "basic method of democracy" on which [it] hoped to build up [a] constitution' (Emphasis added). There are four issues mentioned in relation to each other in this statement: a) the element of reason; b) the fears of a community; c) the 'method' of democracy and d) the making of a constitution. Can fears of a community merely be handled through reason? Does the 'democratic method' rest solely on reason? How can a constitution be envisaged and worked out *a priori* before the issues between communities are settled? Nehru leaves these questions unanswered. In stark contrast to his earlier willingness to sacrifice reason to achieve goodwill, Nehru now takes shelter in the boundaries of reason and finds it in perfect consonance with democracy.

If we look at the case of Kashmir, after Maharaja Hari Singh was finally persuaded to accede to India, Nehru promised a plebiscite. He arrested Sheikh Abdullah unceremoniously in 1953, after exonerating him of the same charges earlier. Nehru first insisted on taking the Kashmir issue to the UN. The Security Council adopted Resolution 122 of 24 January 1957, decreeing [that] both India and Pakistan would ensure 'the final disposition of the state of Jammu and Kashmir...in accordance to the will of the people (to be) expressed through the *democratic method* of a free and impartial plebiscite conducted under the auspices of the United Nations' (Emphasis added). However, the Council overlooked a contentious issue underlying its resolution: How can any 'democratic method' in a historical (and political) dispute get carried out, until the dispute itself has been addressed democratically?

In his telegram to Prime Minister Liaquat Ali Khan on 31 October 1947, Nehru wrote: 'Our assurance that we shall withdraw our troops from Kashmir as soon as peace and order are restored and leave the decision about the future of the State to the people of the State was conditioned with a promise of plebiscite, which was repeated, by high-level leaders as well as Indian representatives in the United Nations.' Nehru was laying down a difficult proposal, where the withdrawal of troops was conditioned upon the atmosphere of peace. Even if he had reasons to suspect Pakistan's designs on Kashmir, it wasn't prudent or democratic of him to allow his suspicions to turn into paranoia. Borders are the nation's paranoia, where reason succumbs to madness. How can the presence of troops be a good premise to bring peace and order? If civil society lives under the shadow of armed men, isn't peace being bought by fear and uncertainty? Is this the precondition of the 'democratic method'? The same Nehruvian logic has stayed on for all these years and become an almost permanent logic of the Indian state, as life and memory lies ravaged in Kashmir.

The limits of Nehru's 'democratic method' were also visible in the case of the Naga demand. It is well known that the Indian Constitution borrowed generously from the Government of India Act, 1935. A colonial mindset was particularly evident in the case of the Assam Disturbed Areas Act, 1955, a predecessor to the more draconian Armed Forces Special Powers Act of 1958. The ADA Act was passed by the Assam Assembly to counter the A.Z. Phizo-led Naga insurgency. It followed the guidelines set by an ordinance passed by the colonial government in August 1942. Ironically, the '42 ordinance was passed to counter the opposition to the war effort by the Congress Party. The Congress now deployed the same law in its frontier states.

On 20 February 1947, the Naga National Council (NNC) sent a memorandum to Lord Mountbatten, then viceroy of India, requesting the British government to set up an interim government for the Nagas for a period of ten years, after which they would freely choose their own form of government. In the backdrop of this extraordinary postcolonial moment of legalistic ironies, Nehru told the NNC delegation led by Phizo, aboard the steamer SS *Lusai* on the river Brahmaputra in Silghat, Assam, on 29 December 1951:

> I consider freedom very precious. I am sure that the Nagas are as free as I am bound by all sorts of laws, the Nagas are not to the same extent bound by such laws and governed by their customary laws and usages. But the independence the Nagas are after, is something quite different from individual or group freedom. In the present context of affairs both in India and the world, it is impossible to consider even for a moment such an absurd demand for independence of the Nagas. It is doubtful whether the Nagas realize the consequences of what they are asking for. For their present demand would ruin them.

Nehru's language and his concern for democracy appear to be under severe strain. The rationalist constrains of territorial nationalism had caught up with his liberal generosity. The Naga demand becomes 'absurd', failing to pass the test of Nehruvian reason. The Nagas will now be governed by the sole, legitimate arbitrator of power, the Indian nation-state. The question of freedom can be posed only within the Indian nationalist 'context'. Democratic values are meaningful only within the framework of law, now part of the accepted colonial legacy inherited by the Indian state. Nehru ends on a paternalistic note, reasoning with the Nagas that this was for their own good. In the border areas of Kashmir and Nagaland, Nehru encountered the frontiers of reason.

Sri Aurobindo was a man hailed by most leading nationalists of his time, across ideologies. But the nationalist thinker,

Aurobindo was most impressed with was perhaps Bal Gangadhar Tilak. Among other things, he significantly praised Tilak for his balance between 'progressive ideas' and 'conservative temperament'. It is interesting that Aurobindo should recognize this paradox in Tilak as exceptional. It throws some light on what Aurobindo regarded as a desirable balance for a nationalist.

In 1936, Aurobindo declined to meet with Jawaharlal Nehru, citing, 'Jawaharlal is coming on a political mission and as president of the Congress, while we have to steer clear not only of politics but of the shadow of politics.' he did not see the ashram as a site for politics the way Gandhi did. Though like Gandhi, Aurobindo believed the ashram to be a place for intense activity. But his project of 'swaraj' (self-rule) was primarily about spiritual regeneration. Gandhi was not only keen to meet Aurobindo in Pondicherry (an event that never took place), but he had also wired him in 1921 with a request to nominate him for the position of president of the upcoming Congress session. Aurobindo declined. He upheld Gandhi's movement of passive resistance (which he had conceived before Gandhi's famous essay on satyagraha was published), but wanted it redefined within masculinist parameters: 'Passive resistance cannot build up a strong and great nation unless it is masculine…We do not want to develop a nation of women who know only how to suffer and not how to strike.'

In contrast, his idea of 'active resistance' against 'illegal and violent methods of coercion' did not involve 'meek submission to illegal outrage'. Gandhi would have agreed to this description of 'active resistance', as his idea of satyagraha was characterized by intense nonviolent activity. Aurobindo however calls for a measured necessity of violence, limited to 'repelling attacks', which does not spill over into 'aggressive resistance.' He believed there could be no compromise regarding the duty of 'national manhood'. The concept of an assertive masculinity is fitted into a gendered idea of the nation as divine mother. It lies at the crux of Aurobindo's national idea.

Aurobindo, however, offers a radical twist to his idea of the nation-as-mother by defining it not in terms of the 'sacred' but in terms of the 'divine'. In an essay on social reforms, Aurobindo talks about the impossibility of recreating certain tenets, which were earlier held 'sacred', in modern times. He writes, 'Manu is no doubt national, but so is the animal sacrifice and the burnt offering. Because a thing is national of the past, it need not follow that it must be national of the future. It is stupid not to recognize altered conditions.' Gandhi says something very similar in *Hind Swaraj*, 'The true dharma is unchanging, while tradition may change with time. If we were to follow some tenets of *Manusmriti*, there would be moral anarchy. We have quietly discarded them altogether.' There is a striking resemblance between Aurobindo's divine/sacred schema and Gandhi's dharma/tradition. If for Gandhi, dharma is eternal and tradition historical, for Aurobindo the idea of the 'sacred' is historical, while the 'divine' is something that, being eternal, always belongs to the future.

Aurobindo looks at the (historical) past both in a concrete and abstract sense, where the 'sacred' is part of a history that is fixed in (its) time, while an underlying 'spirit' of history overflows across time(s). It is in the latter sense that he conceives of the past in 'national' terms, and defines 'sanatana dharma' in terms of the 'spirit' of national history. Nationalism, like sanatana dharma, is 'eternal religion'. Nationalism is both 'God' and 'Nature'; it is divine nature. Aurobindo takes the idea of the nation far beyond its actual, historical invention in the modern west and its transportation to the colonies. He stretches the idea of the nation into the medieval and ancient era from a spiritually imbued, orientalist perspective of a unified cultural ethos, as well as a historical one.

The description is reminiscent of Hegel. '(T)o each nation,' writes Hegel, 'a single principle, comprised under its geographical and anthropological existence.' This principle, to Hegel, is also the 'natural principle', related to both 'spirituality' and 'divine law'. However, the unfolding of this national principle, 'from its undeveloped infancy up to the time when, in the full manhood of free ethical self-consciousness, it presses in upon universal history', is for Hegel a movement within modernity and the development of the modern state. Aurobindo seems to be carving out a slightly more complicated place, between the Hegelian Left and the Hegelian Right. The Hegelian Right considers the nation in teleological terms, as an ideal form of human society and collective destiny. Aurobindo concurs with this idea but diverges from the contention that reason is the only liberating principle of human civilization. 'Life escapes,' he wrote in an essay, 'from the formulas and systems reason labours to impose on it.' Aurobindo was alert to the tyranny and limitation of reason. Truth was vaster than reason, and 'concealed' even from the tall claims of reason. Aurobindo also does not argue, like the Right Hegelians, for an Absolute (restorative) order, where state and orthodox religion converge. Despite being fundamentally interested in the religious principle as a source of human emancipation, Aurobindo develops a dialectic within that principle which borrows from the spirit of a Left Hegelian. This is the dialectic between the 'sacred' and the 'divine', where the 'sacred' holds relevance only specific to its time, while the 'divine' exceeds historical time. The synthesis of the two contrary notions of 'sacred' and 'divine' is however pushed into an unreconciled, unspecified, culturally heterogeneous 'future'. For Aurobindo, the modern condition augurs a facilitating moment for a new, historical reconciliation between faiths.

For Aurobindo the future, in relation to the eternal, shines with a possibility, a promise. It is, for him, concealed in the language of the *Vedas*. But why grant a text the same futurity which is granted to divinity? What makes *Manusmriti* sacred, hence a thing of the past, and the *Vedas* divine, hence a thing of the future?

I will hazard a short answer to this pertinent question. For Aurobindo, the epistemological content of the *Vedas* is a 'concealed' one. He does not give this idea any casteist sanction, but relates it to its future-ness. The other aspect Aurobindo attaches crucial importance to in *The Secret of the Veda* is the element of 'sacrifice'. Delving into the various symbolic aspects of sacrifice, Aurobindo considers the sacrificial moment as the foundational one for the spiritual law of being. It can be compared to Walter Benjamin's idea of 'mythical violence' which is law-founding and blood-spilling, a conservative and restorative form of violence. The idea and act of sacrifice marks a certain ritual and scriptural sanction in the world of the 'divine'. Sacrifice here creates a state of exception where the (norm of) divine law is established by committing a sovereign act of violence. But this law is not entirely understood by Aurobindo as a norm. As he says elsewhere: 'This sanatana dharma has many scriptures, *Veda*, *Vedanta*, *Gita*, *Upanishads*...nor could it reject the *Bible* and the *Koran*; but its real, most authoritative scripture is in the heart in which the Eternal has His dwelling.' Despite giving the *Vedas* a higher scriptural and 'foundational' sanction (and one may ask, is the 'foundation' pure? Is its 'light', uncontaminated by the 'shadow' of caste?), Aurobindo treats it among other such texts in terms of what exceeds these texts. The future of the divine law, one learns from Aurobindo, simply lies in the heart. No text, despite its inclusion in the 'nation's' spiritual history, can guarantee or claim that future.

This 'future', aligned with the 'divine', is integral to

Aurobindo's nationalism. The divine is aligned to the future, towards a law of the future, where specific texts or ideas of the past are to be relinquished. But what is this violence of divine law which is non-textual, non-sacred? What spirit does it embody? Is the divine law a mystical/spiritual law? In 'The Divine Life', Aurobindo finds it as much in material things—life, labour and vitality—as in the spiritual. Divine law seems like an inexhaustible idea or 'force'. For Benjamin, 'divine violence' is violence of pure means, a law-establishing violence which demands bloodless sacrifice and the establishment of (a new) justice. It is both a task and an event. In Aurobindo's case, the 'divine task' is attached to the moment of 'sacrifice', symbolic or real. As an event, Aurobindo retains the idea of both violent and nonviolent sacrifice, defined at a symbolic spiritual level. The idea of 'divine' and 'mythical' violence, as Benjamin differentiates them, appears unresolved in Aurobindo.

In the context of Hindu-Muslim relations, Aurobindo's idea of motherland and nationalism takes sharp political turns. He states categorically, 'Hindu-Mahomedan unity' cannot come from 'political adjustments or Congress flatteries. It must be sought deeper down, in the heart and the mind, for where the causes of disunion are, there the remedies must be sought.' On the same question, while admiring the nationalist spirit of the 'Hindu Sabha', Aurobindo critiqued its 'rivalry with Mahomedan pretensions'. Aurobindo is unhappy with both appeasement and antagonism as political attitudes towards the Muslim community.

Having outlined this firm, preliminary objective, Aurobindo diagnoses the fundamental problem between Hindus and Muslims as one based on 'misunderstanding'. He directs the nation's energies to 'remove the cause of…misunderstanding.' The Hindu's patriotic duty lay in 'unfaltering love' for the Muslims, in whom, says Aurobindo, 'Narayana' dwells and to whom 'our Mother has given a permanent place in her bosom.' So the idea of the nation-as-mother is an inclusive one, not specific to any religious community, and this is because the national community demands a higher unity than religion. For Aurobindo, 'The days of religions are over...none have solved mankind's problems.' The national, for Aurobindo seems to be more futuristic than the religious, in the sense that the religious is merely the sacred and belongs perpetually to the past, while the national is part of the march of divinity, always looking towards the future. It is in this context of the future that Aurobindo places the historical event of the Islamic conquest in India.

For him, the 'real problem' of Muslim rule in India wasn't 'subjection to a foreign rule and the ability to recover freedom, but the struggle between two civilizations.' For Aurobindo, there were 'two conceivable solutions' to this problem. The first was 'a higher spiritual principle' attempted by Akbar and Guru Nanak: Akbar's attempt, a failure, was more 'intellectual and political' than 'spiritual', while Nanak's, though 'universal in principle', ended up as a 'sect in practice'. For Aurobindo to endorse the importance of spiritual thought vis-à-vis its universal scope is rather strange. The second was a 'political patriotism' which went beyond the religious sphere and united the two communities, for which he credits Akbar. But interestingly, he locates the failure of this attempt in the 'common administrative abilities of the two communities'. Aurobindo finds both spiritual and institutional measures lacking in the medieval attempts to unite Hindus and Muslims. But for the future, Aurobindo saw a possible reconcilement in the combination of 'the deepest elements of Islam and Vedanta'. This is a deeply heterogeneous idea compared to Vivekananda's hierarchical division of the 'Vedanta soul and Muslim body'. Aurobindo's idea, in contrast, is closer to Dara

Shikoh's gesture towards an Indo-Islamic tradition. The prince and mystic was among the first to translate *The Upanishads* into Persian.

In the 'nationalist' context of Hindu-Muslim unity, while accepting Hindu-Muslim rivalry as a medieval legacy [and] a symptom of 'British ascendancy', Aurobindo says, he does not 'understand Hindu nationalism as a possibility under modern conditions'. Hindu nationalism made sense to him only during the time of Shivaji and Ramdas, when the 'misuse of their domination by the Mahomedan element was fatal to India's future.' This future, for Aurobindo, seems to be invested in the divine aspect of the nation, where a shared cultural unity and a spirit of toleration may thrive together. This divine spirit, which Aurobindo imagines both in terms of human beings' inner nature and its historical manifestation, is imbued with the idea of a spiritual surplus. The divine, as nature and law, as what exceeds past and present, is our surplus.

'Mahomedan domination,' he writes, 'once tending to Indian unity and toleration, had become oppressive and disruptive.' For Aurobindo, it is not Mahomedan rule in itself which threatened the ethos of Indian nationalism during the medieval era, but its subsequent excesses. But in his time, Aurobindo felt, the idea of 'swadesh' included both Hindus and Muslims. So his 'ideal therefore is an Indian nationalism' rather than a "Hindu nationalism"'. He defined this nationalism as 'largely Hindu in its spirit and traditions,' but 'wide enough also to include the Moslem and his culture and traditions.' It was Aurobindo's belief that through a manly spirit of intensity and brotherhood, Hindus would be able to win swaraj for themselves and, despite resistance from the Muslims, for them as well. He was willing to grant the Hindu Sabha its relevance in modern times, if it would 'direct its whole efforts' towards unity and brotherhood. But if it worked as a 'disruptive' agency, he urged for its rejection. Here too, the desire for the 'inevitable future' moves Aurobindo to seek this reconciliation and brotherhood between the two communities. The idea of the future within Aurobindo's conception of the divine seems to include the idea of reconcilement which is both spiritual and national, and requires the overcoming of history. Aurobindo's suggestion for Hindus and Muslims is to abandon history for the sake of a divinely ordained future.

The Hegelian echo in Aurobindo' idea of a nation-state as divine manifestation, and as the will and spirit of the people, tends to structure the liberating aspect of human destiny and experience within the problem of a nation-power.

~

Rabindranath Tagore grappled with the idea of culture more in aesthetic and civilizational terms. In a 1924 lecture titled 'Civilization and Progress', delivered in China, Tagore says, 'The word "civilization" being a European word, we have hardly yet taken the trouble to find out its real meaning... We ask ourselves, "Has it the same meaning as some word in our own language which denotes for us the idea of human perfection?"' Even though 'civilization' is a European invention, Tagore finds it a translatable word for heterogeneous cultures which also resonates with the universal possibility of 'human perfection'. Tagore acknowledges that the idea of perfection, for a 'complex' being like man, capable of 'transcending himself...cannot be crystallized into an inflexible idea.' The idea of perfection is both universal and singular, as different races have evolved 'different shades of definition.' Despite admitting to the various 'shades' of cultural translatability, Tagore always refused to entertain any idea which was less than universal.

It was precisely on this ground that, despite his admiration for Gandhi, Tagore refused to accept his idea of swaraj, as much as his political strategies like non-cooperation and the boycott of foreign goods. In a letter to Gandhi, Tagore asks, 'What is *Swaraj*? It is maya, it is like a mist, that will vanish leaving no stain on the radiance of the Eternal. However we may delude ourselves with the phrases learnt from the West, *Swaraj* is not our objective.' Further in the letter, Tagore addresses his disagreements about non-cooperation: 'The idea of non-cooperation is political asceticism. Our students are bringing their offering of sacrifices to what? Not to a fuller education but to non-education. It has at its back a fierce joy of annihilation...No, in its passive moral form is asceticism and in its active moral form is violence. The desert is as much a form of a *himsa* as is the raging sea in storms, they both are against life.' Tagore was against the idea of renunciation, in life as much as in politics. The idea of a 'fuller education' for Tagore, as he writes in *The Religion of Man*, is 'the preparation for a complete life of man'. The 'complete life' is a life of 'perfect harmony' with the world, which is also the 'grand harmony of the universal'.

The idea of the universal in Tagore comes from an elaborate understanding of human nature, culture and the aim of human consciousness. It is part of Tagore's 'philosophical anthropology'. Mohinder Singh explores this aspect in his essay, 'Tagore on Modernity, Nationalism and "the Surplus in Man"', on the poet-thinker's key concepts of community, nation and civilization.

Tagore uses analogous phrases for 'human nature', like 'inner nature', 'aesthetic nature', 'moral nature' and 'true nature'. In contrast to animal life, trapped within the 'unimaginative repetition of life within a safe restriction imposed by Nature', human beings have the 'responsibility to outlive [their] life in order to live in truth.' The idea of truth is an extension of the idea of nature. Truth is not *merely* nature; the latter is merely animal nature. Nature restricts life with limitations and patterns which are visible in animal life. Human life has been bestowed with the possibility of unearthing the meaning of nature, from where all meaning emanates. Tagore clarifies, 'what we call nature is not a philosophical abstraction, not cosmos, but what is revealed to man as nature.' The meaning of nature and of human evolution, revealed to the 'consciousness of self', are 'revelations of a great meaning, the self-expression of a truth.'

Truth adds to the evolution of (human) nature, 'a value… that cannot be measured or analysed.' Truth is an incalculable value. As Tagore suggests, this value manifests itself through our consciousness 'in science, philosophy and the arts, [and] in social ethics.' In all these disciplines of knowledge, the key element for Tagore is their universality. Welcoming the universal aspects of cultural modernity, he acknowledges a 'surplus' in man. He goes on to establish the three characteristics of this surplus. One, it is a surplus denied to animals, therefore unique to the human species. Two, man is in 'the possession of a Spirit' with an 'enormous capital with a surplus far in excess of…the animal in man'. This is an extension of the first contention, where the idea of human capital is regarded by Tagore as the source of its creative surplus.

Such a view, in consonance with Hegel, treats the idea of surplus as a (metaphysical and creative) human property and as something the human being owns *in potentia*. Three, surplus contributes to 'world-spirit'. Tagore accords an angelic status to the idea of surplus in the aristocratic sphere of 'leisure', calling it the 'Angel of Surplus'. This Angel fosters 'detachment from the compelling claim of physical need'. Tagore's surplus works at the level of the universal, the spiritual and the aesthetic, by acknowledging these three spheres as capable of fostering the true possibilities of the human being. The 'surplus' of man, *revealed* through art, spirituality, science, philosophy, ethics and leisure, are expressions of the inner nature of human beings. Tagore's idea of the nature of being, of a being revealed through nature, is that of a creative unfolding of the spirit.

To make a fruitful digression, Karl Marx's idea of the 'surplus' differs from Tagore's. Marx treats the value of surplus (or surplus value) in purely materialist terms, as excess value created by labour that is appropriated by the capitalist and denied to the labourer. Surplus value, in the Marxian sense, is both quantifiable in terms of money and unquantifiable in terms of life and time. It is value produced by labour which is exploited by the owners of capital. Unlike the idea of surplus value as human property, Marx defines it as the property of labour. If we include a structural understanding, Tagore's creative surplus of art and leisure is largely possible for those privileged enough to not have the surplus they create exploited, their life reduced to mere subsistence. The 'enormous capital' (Tagore) of realizing one's surplus value requires ownership of material luxury, denied to those who sell their labour for a pittance. But the meaning of surplus value need not be understood *only* within relations of material production.

Jacques Rancière has shown in *Nights of Labour*, workers in nineteenth century Paris were audaciously dreaming, drawing metaphysical meanings from life and producing journalistic literature and poetry. They dared to conceive a world beyond limitations posed by their class situation or work hours. These archived narratives, memorably brought to life by Rancière, give credence to the wider idea of surplus. Marx too, in *The German Ideology*, describes the communist society to come as one where 'nobody has one exclusive sphere of activity' and makes it possible for someone to hunt in the morning, go fishing in the afternoon and be a critic after dinner. Marx suggests a diverse capacity of human activity that seems akin to Tagore and Hegel's idea of the creative surplus of human beings.

Tagore's idea of 'world-spirit' also has an affinity with German Romanticism, particularly with the idea of a world-creating spirit propounded by Friedrich Schelling, of a creative and eternal spirit as an expression and double of nature, a unity of consciousness. It is, however, first necessary to understand its philosophical and political differences with Hegel. The German philosopher locates the limits of Indian philosophy in its inability to conceive of freedom in concrete, determinate terms in relation to the individual subject of history. The 'Spirit', according to Hegel, in its essence, substance and truth, is freedom and 'the Idea of freedom' is the 'essence of Spirit and absolutely final purpose of history'. The Greeks had 'splendid liberty' but denied it to slaves and women. It was left to the great destiny of the 'Germanic peoples...through Christianity', to discover 'that man as man is free and that freedom of Spirit is the very essence of man's nature.'

However, Hegel denies this character in Oriental thought, claiming that, 'Orientals do not yet know that Spirit—Man as such—is free. And because they do not know it, they are not free.' He finds in this lack the reason why India, despite being 'so rich in spiritual products of greatest profundity, has no history.' Hegel critiques Oriental philosophy's inability to distinguish between Nature and Spirit. For him, this is the reason behind the lack of universality in the history of the Orient, as the substance of universality is based on the individual subject and its capacity for freedom. It is the *actual* freedom of man, embodied in the individual subject, which is singularly capable of universality. This universality consists of both Nature, which is everlasting, and Spirit, which is produced in history. In Indian philosophy, universality fails to develop a solid (historical) ground for a concrete idea of universality to exist. The manifestation of the universal in the state is what Hegel says constitutes, 'the culture of a nation.' Before Indians had a state of their own, after the departure of the British, they were merely a part of 'prehistory' without any concrete consciousness of freedom.

From an Upanishadic perspective, Tagore believes 'what we call nature is not a philosophical abstraction, not cosmos, but what is revealed to man as nature.' The understanding of nature is not a matter of reflection but of deep experience. He further says, man's 'religion tried to gain a perfect communion with the mysterious magic of Nature's forces through his own power of magic.' The relationship between man and nature is drawn in alchemic terms. This thought is profoundly different from modern, rationalist thought, and closer to the Jena Romantics. Tagore's idea of nature is affirmatively Orientalist, in the sense that the poet-philosopher is consciously steering away from rationalist thought. Referring to an unmentioned verse in the *Upanishads*, Tagore understands universality as 'the surrender of our individual self to the Universal Self'. This falls precisely into Hegel's problem with Oriental philosophy.

Tagore calls the 'individual mind' an 'isolated freak', and makes the point that a 'civilization perishes in which the individual thwarts the revelation of the universal.' In Tagore's understanding, the individual attains the 'freedom of social relationship...through owning responsibility to his community, thus gaining its collective power for his own welfare.' The individual is understood in relation to, and as a part of, the community. It is the community which makes the individual and not vice-versa. Tagore further argues that 'in the social or political field, the lack of freedom is based upon the spirit of alienation.' Pure individual freedom is understood as a *lack* in social or community ties. In an extraordinary paragraph, Tagore clarifies his position on the ethical relationship between the individual and society, where Hegel's preferred equation between individual and community is seen differently:

> One may imagine that an individual who succeeds in dissociating himself from his fellows attains real freedom, inasmuch as all ties of relationship imply obligation to others. But we know that, though it may sound paradoxical, it is true that in the human world only a perfect arrangement of interdependence gives rise to freedom. The most individualistic of human beings who own no responsibility are the savages who fail to attain their fullness of manifestation. They live immersed in obscurity, like an ill-lighted fire that cannot liberate itself from its envelope of smoke. Only those who have the power to cultivate mutual understanding and cooperation may attain their freedom from the segregation of an eclipsed life. The history of the growth of freedom is the history of the perfection of human relationship.

The individual is ethically defined as one who fulfils his 'obligation to others'. Freedom is defined within a certain idea of the perfectibility in human relationships. Is Tagore, by endorsing a social idea of ethics, promoting a conservative idea of community? Is the community, in Tagore's idea, the absolute social locus of the 'Universal Self' where the individual must sacrifice and surrender? To answer these questions, it is necessary to make another small detour of Hegel.

For Hegel, the universal (or universality) cannot 'originate within the ethical community'. The ethical community must have a 'higher universality, which makes it *disunited in itself*' (Emphasis added). Hegel argues that for any community to progress ethically it needs to abolish its particularity to reach a 'higher' universal. This is the objective leap of a determinate community of individuals into the 'world-historical' realm. Such a leap is of course determined by the dynamic process of history. It ensures, for Hegel, the onward march of national destiny.

While Tagore's idea of universality is also pursued by the idea of a higher aim, its movement is more critical and complicated than Hegel's. Tagore writes, 'The limited boundaries of a race or a country within which the supreme truth of humanity has been more or less realized in the past are crossed to-day from the outside. The countries are physically brought closer to each other by science.' Tagore argues against cultural territoriality, contextualizing the universal very specifically against the spread of science. He repudiates the idea of national communities in scathing terms: 'The primitive barbarity of limitless suspicion and mutual jealousy fills the world's atmosphere today, the barbarity of the aggressive individualism of nations, pitiless in its greed, unashamed of its boastful brutality.'

The individualist form of nationalism which Hegel finds liberating is, for Tagore, a relapse into primitivism, where the ethical community can no longer exist. He goes deeper into the matter: 'Those that have come out for depredation in this universal night have the indecent audacity to say that such conditions are eternal in man, that the moral ideals are only for individuals but that the race belongs to the primitive nature of the animal.' He reads a contradiction into the moral claims of modern individualism, warning that the promises of universalism end up in spiritual alienation. Making a radical, anti-Enlightenment gesture, Tagore blames certain attitudes brought about by science for bringing in this night: 'But science has not brought with it the light that helps understanding. On the contrary science on its practical side has raised obstacles... against the development of a sympathetic knowledge.' This diverges starkly, and firmly, from the Hegelian idea of progress and universalism. The instrumentality of science has brought darkness instead of light, removing the ethical element of empathy for others.

Tagore finds a certain mischief that makes 'its entry through this back-door of utility'. The utilitarian aspect of modern science introduced the larger impulse of dealing with questions of progress and happiness, which seeped into the very psyche that produced the exploitative logic of colonialism. The 'civilizing mission' went hand in hand with the promotion of the idea of progress. Classical utilitarianism, as propounded by James Mill and John Stuart Mill, often provided justificatory arguments for the exploitative claims of colonial empires. On the one hand, the utilitarian thinkers argued for the maximization of happiness, and on the other, stood by racial differences and the necessity of colonial governance to civilize the barbarians of the colonies.

Tagore was intuitively aware of this game. He realises that the principle of utility was injected into the nationalist spirit to introduce a competing idea of sovereignty and freedom. Tagore finds his idea of deep, human universalism at odds with this idea of national self-determination. What desirable idea of universalism does he pit it against? In his words, 'The Spirit of Love, dwelling in the boundless realm of the surplus, emancipates our consciousness from the illusory bond of the separateness of self; it is ever trying to spread its illumination in the human world.' So we are back to the special and unique idea of 'surplus' in Tagore: the surplus of love which negates the surplus of commodities that negate it. It is the spirit of this surplus that Tagore pits against the determinate, narrow universalism of nation and its idea of culture. Tagore is not against the flowering of the individual, which for Hegel determines the course of human freedom. But he is critically aware of the modern structures of life that limit the individual. In his essay, 'Personality', Tagore writes, 'It is the rampant materialism of the present age which ruthlessly sacrifices individuals to the bloodthirsty idols of organization.'

Tagore's critique of the individual is two-fold, as one who

tends to selfishly resist ethical obligations, and one who is also an easy prey to the instrumental lures of modern civilization and politics and hence, isn't the proper subject of universalism. This assumption made Tagore extremely reluctant to accept Gandhi's project of swaraj, as he saw in it a self-fashioning that stubbornly refuses the promise of universalism in the encounter with Europe. In this, Tagore echoed Nehru who did not believe in the clash of cultures and, as Octavio Paz pointed out, saw the East-West opposition in historical terms.

Gandhi's idea of self-rule as a corollary of self-abnegation and self-sacrifice was not an attractive proposition for Tagore. He was also unhappy with the charkha: 'The charkha in its proper place can do no harm but will rather do much good. But where, by reasoned failure to acknowledge the differences in man's temperament it is in the wrong place, there thread can only be spun at the cost of a great deal of the mind itself. Mind is no less valuable than cotton thread.' Tagore was anxious that the singular idea of self-sustainability behind Gandhi's choice of the charkha was a dangerous practice towards cultural self-isolation. To accord a central place to the practice of spinning, taking it out of its 'proper place', meant for Tagore that Gandhi was replacing intellectual activity with a non-intellectual one. Self-rule as a political ideal suffers, in Tagore's view, from a distorted move towards self-fortification. For Tagore, 'erecting barricades of fierce separateness in the name of national necessity is offering hindrance' to the emancipatory project of 'the spiritual Man'. Tagore's spiritual man is a culturally boundless being, and since the spirit of cultures cannot be marked by territories, the spiritual man is beyond the political loyalties demanded by nationalism.

For Tagore, the East-West conflict is a result of mutual misunderstanding in the cultural realm. He explains in a letter, 'The West has misunderstood the East which is at the root of the disharmony that prevails between them, but will it mend the matter if the East in her turn tries to misunderstand the West?...We from the East have to come to her to learn whatever she has to teach us; for by doing so we hasten the fulfillment of this age.' Was the political aspect behind the cultural encounter between the colonized and the colonizer, simply to be understood through the Romantic idea of harmony between East and West?

Tagore's idea of culture, in contrast to Nehru's, is not only non-national, but goes a critical step further—it is vehemently anti-national. It is interesting that a poet, among all modern Indian thinkers, had thought most fiercely against nationalism. In his famous essay, 'Nationalism and the West', Tagore asserts that the 'goal of human history' had nothing to do with 'the fierce self-idolatry of nation-worship'. But Tagore also called nationalism the 'collective self-interest of a whole people'. This paradox clarifies how, for Tagore, nationalism is not only narcissistic but also ungenerous and downright selfish. He never placed culture within the framework of nationalism. He made a distinction between the 'Spirit of the West' and the 'Nation of the West'. The 'spirit' is spoken of in glowing terms. Tagore praises the 'simple and the natural man' of medieval Europe who, 'with all his violent passions and desires, was engaged in trying to find out a reconciliation in the conflict between the flesh and the spirit.' He saluted the British for producing 'great-hearted men, thinkers of great thoughts', for giving 'rise to a great literature.' The 'Nation of the West' in contrast, is a 'mechanical organization'.

Tagore evokes a literary and artistic idea of the 'spirit', securing it from the mercantile spirit of Europe that was responsible for its colonial enterprise. This was however an uncritical affirmation of European Romanticism, a movement that produced a great creative and intellectual force, declared the free expression of ideas and feelings, and critiqued Enlightenment rationality and the Industrial Revolution. It argued for a passionate return to 'nature' and affirmed the 'heroic individual'. However, Romanticism also sought a return to European medievalism. Its nostalgic notions of a folklorish past wove these fantasies into ideas of nationhood. From folklore to epics, the Romantic texts were deployed to serve the resurgent nationalism in Germany and Central Europe.

In Romanticism, the critique of Enlightenment rationality went overboard, affirming values that fed cultural revivalism. The idea of collective self-expression, which framed the idea of romantic nationalism, is what Isaiah Berlin called 'political romanticism'. Romanticism's conflict with reason was not outside the problem of imagining a nation, just as the idea of a 'people' in the French Revolution also veered around remaking a national community. The problem with all national communities is their creation of the other. Every nation has minorities, and their history and relationship with the nation has been uneasy.

In the same essay, Tagore writes, 'We had known the hordes of Moghals and Pathans who invaded India...as human races [but] we had never known them as a nation'. He draws attention to how a political relationship with the other, when mediated by the ideology of the nation, takes on a different meaning altogether. He rues the loss of a direct, unmediated relationship. The nation is understood as a juridical form of power, in the shape of an 'octopus of abstractions.' In a Gandhian spirit, Tagore said the nation was a 'power loom' compared to other forms of power which were 'hand looms'. The nation here is seen to be as impersonal as a machine. He compares 'government by the Nation' with shoes—'It regulates our steps with a closed up system'—that pinch and suffocate the wearer. To him, the English nation is 'neither British nor anything else'; it is 'an applied science'. He fiercely believes that a nation is not even a cultural byproduct of science, but a form of applied technology. The nation is an organized name of 'politics and commerce' that disturbs the 'harmony of higher social life.'

Tagore furthers his argument on not retaining the East-Went dichotomy in essentialist terms: '...we have to consider that the West is *necessary* to the East. We are complementary to each other because of our different outlooks upon life which have given us different aspects of truth. Therefore if it be true that the spirit of the West has come upon our fields in the *guise* of a storm it is all the same scattering living seeds that are immortal. And when in India we shall be able to assimilate in our life *what is permanent* in Western civilization we shall be in the position to bring about a reconciliation of these two great worlds' (Emphasis added). East and West are both fragments of the truth, and as fragments they hold two different versions of the truth, whose reconciliation is a matter of cultural and spiritual necessity. The modern civilization of the West is a mere disguise, which has to be ripped apart in order to discover the *other* West which holds values that transcend the cruel limitations of history.

Tagore further asks the question: 'Of all things in Western civilization, those which this Western Nation has given us in a most generous measure are law and order. But is not this order merely a negative good?' Contrast this to the speech given by India's ex-Prime Minister, Mahmohan Singh, at Oxford on 8 July 2005, after receiving an honorary degree of Doctor of Civil Law, where he praised the 'beneficial consequences' of British colonial administration for introducing 'the rule of law, of a constitutional government, of a free press, of a professional civil service, of modern universities and research laboratories.' Tagore's ethical caution disappears in Singh's neoliberal hindsight, as he pays his due to the colonial legacy that served him.

Tagore lays down a more concrete political critique of colonial domination, 'The present struggle is being waged against compulsory cooperation, against one-sided combination, against the armed imposition of modern methods of exploitation, masquerading under the name of civilisation.' He is aware that the exploitative relationship which marks colonial rule distorts the grounds on which even the most confident class among the colonized can dream of universal knowledge. The discourse of universality and humanity carries the Eurocentric stains of a Hegelian Enlightenment. Its sense of superiority is writ large on the presumptions offering singular pride of place to the West in defining humanity and universality.

The pedagogical discourse of the West, eulogizing its contributions to ideas of government and politics, as much as to philosophy, art and literature, and to the idea of civilization itself, is impossible to accept without a sincere belief in one's own inferiority. Part of the intellectual and creative task of the colonized has been to refute their inferiority and challenge the West on its own grounds. Many of these challenges have come by turning Western principles around against their exploitative regimes and not against those principles, themselves. For these reasons, it was rather odd for Tagore, like Nehru, to find colonialism a good time for the production of knowledge and creative inspiration.

For completely dismissing the idea of the nation and nationalism, Tagore can surely be regarded as one of the boldest political thinkers in India. His is a rejection of one of the most central and critically accepted ideas of Western modernity. It is interesting how he rejects the relation between progress and nation, and understands the relationship between the individual and community by considering a higher universal which does not treat the national community as a legitimate—'determinate' in Hegelian terms—ethical ground where the idea of freedom gets enhanced. In both these aspects, Tagore places the question of ethics and freedom of the spirit, not in an affirmation, but in a rejection of the nation.

―

In *Hind Swaraj*, Gandhi lays down the difference between India and Europe in civilizational terms as a conflict between modernity and morality. He goes on to say that 'true civilization' is in fact Indian, as against the 'immoral civilization' of the West: 'The tendency of Indian civilization is to elevate the moral being, that of the Western civilization is to propagate immorality. The latter is godless, the former is based on a belief in God. So understanding and so believing, it behooves every lover of India to cling to the old Indian civilization even as a child clings to its mother's breast.' The distinction between the West and India, as drawn by Gandhi, is Orientalism-in-reverse. The ethnocentric Orientalist dichotomy is posed in the traditionalist terms of 'morality' versus 'immorality'. The West, being modern, is also materialistic, and hence immoral. India is spiritual and hence moral. The inferiorized spiritual essence of the East is held superior to the scientific civilization of the West.

For Gandhi, there exists a cultural route through which modern Europe and India can ethically interact, but that would require an abandoning of the modern ways of life by the European and embrace the religious way of life which India was apparently leading. Gandhi seems to understand colonial power in terms of modern needs and believed that religious civilizations could not have the same impulses. He concludes: 'East and West can only and really meet when the West has thrown overboard modern civilization, almost in its entirety. They can also seemingly meet when the East has also adopted modern civilization. But that meeting would be an armed truce, even as it is between, say, Germany and England, both of which nations are living in the Hall of Death in order to avoid being devoured, the one by the other.'

For Gandhi, the choice was relative and absolute. There was a similarity in the spiritual domains of the erstwhile Christian West and the East. So a spiritual-spiritual relationship between the West and India, where the West debunks its modernity and upholds Christian values, was acceptable to Gandhi.

Gandhi's debate with Tagore occurs in the backdrop of these ideas. To Tagore's accusation that his idea of cultural resistance against the British was a denial of the universal spirit, Gandhi famously said, 'I want the cultures of all the lands to be blown about my house as freely as possible. But I refuse to be blown off my feet by any.' One can easily notice Gandhi's characteristic stubbornness. To Tagore's alarm at Gandhi's call for non-cooperation and the sidelining of the English language, he once again gave a polemical response, focusing on the utilitarian and ideological aspects of English: 'The Poet does not know perhaps that English is today studied because of its commercial and so-called political value.' Adding a sociological observation, he said, 'I know families in which English is being made the mother tongue.' But Gandhi knew Tagore was against all forms of abnegation: 'He has a horror of everything negative. His whole soul seems to rebel against the negative commandments of religion.' He explains his position on non-cooperation to Tagore with fine clarity,

> In my humble opinion, rejection is as much an ideal as the acceptance of a thing. It is as necessary to reject untruth as it is to accept truth. All religions teach that two opposite forces act upon us and that the human endeavour consists in a series of eternal rejections and acceptances. Non-cooperation with

evil is as much a duty as co-operation with good. I venture to suggest that the Poet has done an unconscious injustice to Buddhism in describing nirvana as merely a negative state.

Gandhi makes a fair criticism regarding Tagore's facile understanding of the 'negative' in Buddhism. He goes on to affirm the power of the negative by offering his variation of negation in action, a politics of no-saying, but an active and intense politics nonetheless: 'I...think that the Poet has been unnecessarily alarmed at the negative aspect of Non-cooperation. We had lost the power of saying "no". It had become disloyal, almost sacrilegious to say "no" to the Government. This deliberate refusal to cooperate is like the necessary weeding process that a cultivator has to resort to before he sows.' Gandhi argues that the idea of swaraj, by embodying the self's ability to say no to power, establishes an idea of the self that formulates—and becomes itself through—dissent. Satyagraha was a non-doing in its negativity, or an undoing of a certain kind of politics, a refusal to act violently under provocation; while in its very act of doing so it was a positivity—an expression of one's presence in the world, of confronting violence with concrete acts of non-violence. Gandhi's political ethics lie within this double pull of withdrawal and expression.

In response to Tagore's critique, Gandhi further explains the political context of the movement: 'Our Non-cooperation is neither with the English nor with the West! Our Non-cooperation is with the system the English have established, with the material civilisation and its attendant greed and exploitation of the weak. Our Non-cooperation is a retirement within ourselves.' In its specificity, non-cooperation in Gandhi's formulation is posed against the very problem which Tagore highlights as the crude, exploitative and utilitarian culture of British colonialism. It was not a total rejection of the West or of Western culture, as Tagore had envisaged in his great sense of alarm. Gandhi in fact extends Tagore's moral concerns, by positing non-cooperation as a political as well as ethical response of no-saying to the colonial exploitation of India in the name of providing the goods of progress.

The Gandhian engagement with (colonial) power has a lot to do with evolving a practice which contributes to counter-hegemonic self-making. Tagore's critique of Gandhi's use of the charkha overlooks this aspect. Since Tagore's attitude to world-culture is that of a critical assimilationist, he is anxious about Gandhi's project. For Gandhi, however, spinning was the leading activity at the site of his politics: the ashram. Gandhi's conceived the ashram as an experiment to tackle modernity and its pervasive social imaginaries. The ashram occupied—in its imagination and practice—an in-between place. It was neither bourgeois family nor revolutionary commune. It belonged neither to a sect nor to a party. The ashram was also a space to erase prejudices of caste and manual scavenging. Among the practices of the ashram, the delicate but relentless act of spinning was central. 'There is an art that kills and an art that gives life,' wrote Gandhi in *Young India* on 11 August 1921.

It was not just the idea of self-sufficiency that Gandhi associated with the spinning wheel. The spinning wheel meant attending to a work that appeared boring without any sense of boredom, labouring for a pleasure without privilege, simply doing one's work which consists of a single motion, work that is monotonous and singular. Spinning is not only an activity but also a space, where the task of rotating a simple machine and weaving cloth out of it takes place. Threads are the fruit of the labour and the source of joy. One never produces much thread in a day even after hours of spinning. There is an anti-capitalist imbalance between doing and producing, as much as between time and production. Gandhi was not merely producing cloth to sustain a home-grown industry and the idea of self-sufficiency, but producing a specific relation between time and work in the process. The idea of giving 'life' by spinning cloth implied a self-regenerative process, where a certain self-fashioning was taking place.

On 28 March 1945, Gandhi wrote in *Sevagram*, 'Do spin and spin after due deliberation..."Due deliberation" means realization that charkha or act of spinning is the symbol of non-violence. Ponder; it will be self-evident.'

The act of spinning was an act of deliberation, an act of the will. It was a will to be nonviolent. As an activity of deliberation, spinning was also the opposite of the idea of provocation. Gandhi spun in the face of provocations during the anti-colonial movement—not simply as a political message to his opponents and to power, but to create a space where the self-at-work can be sovereign within that activity. The charkha created a space for negotiating with power. Gandhi realized that the only way to challenge colonial power was by creating a place where the self could announce its own sovereignty, its own will and a strength to produce for itself. It symbolized the soul of satyagraha, which was also an act of protest against the devious means of the colonial regime to have a claim over our time, will, means of sustenance, and sovereignty.

The philosopher Jean Filliozat says in a discussion with the French ethical thinker, Emmanuel Levinas, and Jean Wahl: 'Gandhi treats the question of violence as the primary problem. On the one hand, he supposes—with the whole of Indian civilization—that the enemy of violence is not another violence; violence opposed is not the opposite of violence. On the other hand, the putting into question of the I in the presence of the Other is justified from the general Indian point of view, in any case from the point of view which Gandhi inherits, without being a philosopher himself, in a completely different way to the one that you [Levinas] spoke about.' Gandhi's idea of nonviolence an everyday contact with and struggle against violence. It is by this everyday negotiation violence that he strove to bring a measure of nonviolence into the world.

In *Hind Swaraj*, Gandhi defines history as 'a record of every interruption of the even working of the force of love or of the soul'. Against this biased view of history, Gandhi erects a modern parable against modernity, and a violent legal discourse of history: 'Two brothers quarrel; one of them repents and re-awakens the love that was lying dormant in him; the two again begin to live in peace; nobody takes note of this. But if the two brothers, through the intervention of solicitors or some other reason take up arms or go to law...their doings would be immediately noticed in the Press, they would be the talk of their neighbours, and would probably go down in history. And what is true of families and communities is true of nations,' This passage makes Partha Chatterjee conclude that, for Gandhi, history 'does not record the Truth. Truth lies outside history; it is universal, unchanging. Truth has no history of its own.'

Gandhi contrasts the dominant idea of history with a notion of history based on the 'force of love' and 'the force of the soul or truth'. Gandhi gives a sense of this *other* history by the Gujarati phrase: 'It so happened'. Ajay Skaria has drawn our attention to Gandhi's distinction between the historicity of history on the one hand and 'itihaas' on the other, by using the historicity of satyagraha or even 'satya' as a point of departure. Skaria reads it as Gandhi's indication of the emergence of a 'social history' as against the history of wars. Satyagraha, involving the 'sacrifice of the self', offered a new mode of politics to this counter-historical movement. Sacrifice of the self is the surplus of Gandhian politics. But it is a surplus *within* the sphere of the political, demanding a moral response from the opponent. Partha Chatterjee deplores how this move negates Gandhi's own 'powerful moral critique of the existing state of politics' by ultimately trying to save 'Truth by escaping from politics'. But truth for Gandhi is rather *founded* in that *disjuncture* between morality and politics. The disjuncture between morality and politics is political, and politics is born out of this disjunction. Sacrifice was Gandhi's only conceivable, moral option against the violence of politics.

Manubahen called Gandhi, the man who 'knitted India into a nation'. The term 'nation' however remains a scarce and insignificant signifier in Gandhi's writing. His central preoccupation was to ensure moral progress of the community. Gandhi's politics entails outward expression of inner self-activity. In its wider, nationalist manifestation, he meant to 'knit' this spiritual and social self-activity into national life. As he wrote in *Harijan* (6 October, 1946): 'I felt compelled to come into the political field because I found I could not do even social work without touching politics. I feel that political work must be looked upon in terms of social and moral progress. *In democracy no fact of life is untouched by politics*' (Emphasis added). It was a remarkable statement suggesting the bio-political nature of modern democracy. If (national) politics had a claim over life, self-sovereignty alone could best negotiate with such a power.

Gandhi undertook many activities to define his role in the national movement against British rule. One was Gandhi's many marches that began in earnest on 12 March 1930, when he led a march from the Sabarmati Ashram to the coastal village of Dandi. Its purpose was to break the colonial government's tax law on salt production, by producing salt from seawater. The march was understood as a form of civil disobedience, but like all things Gandhian, it was transformed into his political vocabulary of Salt Satyagraha, where truth and nonviolence made an appearance in politics. It was an active demonstration of Gandhi's language of politics, whose larger aim was swaraj. As an act of nonviolent defiance of governmental law, this instance of Gandhian politics was both affirmative and non-aggressive. It was understood henceforth as a movement that would defy the government on its own terms, and force governmental power to grapple with its unique language.

Gandhi's fasts to quell Hindu-Muslim animosity were politically honest. They operated directly against the interests of Hindu communalism. What Gandhi failed to do for the question of caste, he managed, at least in intent, for the Hindu-Muslim question. His brave 'experiment' in Noakhali, touring the area and calming communal tensions, managed to heal a few hearts. In Gandhi's defence, he had put his ethical politics of tempting violence with nonviolence and risking death to its most radical test. He did not abandon the nonviolent method, which was the more ethical means to adopt against the pragmatic calculations of success. The failure of Gandhian politics reveals the limitations of a violent nationalism which found its logical end in the genocide of Partition.

~

To stay awake night and day—at night for the day and in the day thinking of the night to come.

—Michel Foucault

The failure of the Gandhi–Jinnah talks and the rejection of the Rajaji formula (between July and October 1944) by Muhammad Ali Jinnah, the president of the Muslim League, had immediate repercussions. The League launched the infamous Direct Action Day for the creation of Pakistan on 16 August 1946. Under the shadowy supervision of the League's

Chief Minister in Bengal, H.S. Suhrawardy, riots were allowed to spread across Calcutta. The population in Noakhali was 18 per cent Hindu and 82 per cent Muslim (though landed proprietors were mostly Hindus). A one-sided onslaught started on 10 October, the day of Lakshmi puja. Nirmal Kumar Bose informs that a telegram came from Gandhi to Satish Chandra Dasgupta (a Gandhian who had set up an ashram called the Khadi Pratisthan in Sodepur in 1921), instructing him to send volunteers to Noakhali and assess the state of affairs.

In New Delhi, Gandhi was already considering the question of dying in Noakhali. He wrote in a letter: 'There is an art of dying...As it is, all die, but one has to learn by practice how to die a beautiful death. The matter will not be settled even if everybody went to Noakhali and got killed.' Gandhi said his 'technique of non-violence was on trial' in Noakhali and that it 'remained to be seen how it would answer in the face of the present crisis.' At Kazirkhil, on his way to Srirampur, Gandhi drafted a note for Satish Chandra Dasgupta, where he said with touching clarity: 'I find myself in the midst of exaggeration and falsity. I am unable to discover the truth. There is terrible mutual distrust. Oldest friendships have snapped. Trust and Ahimsa by which I swear and which have to my knowledge sustained me for sixty years, seem to fail.' He touches on the root of the ethical crisis. The breakdown of trust had let loose a sordidly violent atmosphere in Bengal. At Srirampur, Gandhi admitted: 'It is very clear to me that my mere word carries very little weight. Distrust has gone too deep for exhortation.'

These observations show that Gandhi had come to Bengal without any thought of doing politics, but to nevertheless find out the state of politics. He found to his horror and dismay that the only politics he was capable of launching, the politics of truth or satyagraha, was extremely difficult in the circumstances. Despite the odds being heavily against him, Gandhi took trustful steps. In his speech at the prayer meeting in Chandipur, he said to the largely Hindu audience that though they were deceived before by assurances from the state government, it was 'beneath one's dignity to distrust a man's word without sufficient reason. If all Muslims were liars, Islam could not have been a true religion.' However, when Chief Minister Suhrawardy tried to bypass a charge against his government regarding a murder case, saying there were many versions of the story and even he was being accused of complicity in the matter, Gandhi lost his temper and denounced Suhrawardy, saying, 'Yes, you are responsible not only for that murder but for every life lost in Bengal, whether Hindu or Muslim.'

Between October 1946 and January 1948, Nirmal Kumar Bose writes with Foucauldian acumen, Gandhi reached 'two climaxes...simultaneously in his life; one in the personal, spiritual sphere, and the other in the sphere of his public and political relations. Although the two might seem to be unrelated, there was an underlying bond between the two.' The 'two climaxes' refer to Gandhi's controversial experiment of 'brahmacharya' with Manu by night, and by day, his intense activities of satyagraha to quell the communal atmosphere in Noakhali. Gandhi wrote to Jayasukhlal, father of his grandniece Manu, from Calcutta on 4 November, making an authoritative wish: 'Manu's place can be nowhere else but here by my side.' This 'moved me deeply,' Manu confessed. She woke her father in the middle of the night and he advised her to write to Gandhi. Manu wrote to her granduncle 'explicitly laying down the condition' under which she was willing to join him. She made it clear she didn't want to join Gandhi if he sent her away to some other village and didn't allow her to be near him. She promised to 'brave any danger' that might befall her in Noakhali. Gandhi accepted Manu's proposal and asked her to join him on his own condition: Manu would have to participate, with all the risks involved, 'in this great drama of self-sacrifice.'

On Manu's arrival Gandhi told her, according to Bose, that 'He was thinking of a bold and original experiment, whose "heat will be great".' Gandhi explained to Jayasukhlal that he considered 'this Hindu–Muslim unity problem an altar of self-sacrifice. Not a trace of impurity can pass muster here. If there is even a speck of it in Manu, she will fail and go to pieces.' Gandhi's brahmacharya experiment was supposed to purify the aggressors.

Ashwini Tambe finds 'Gandhi's vision of the ideal "public"… an enlarged projection of his purified self.' According to Tambe, Gandhi 'saw his own experiments with diet and sex as literally applicable to all in the nation.' She concludes that, for Gandhi, his 'body represented the body politic.' The intensification in the relationship between Gandhi's own body and the body politic appears to be not only psychic, religious and moral in its manifestations but also material, where the body practices the art and technology of brahmacharya as a means of attaining perfection. But perhaps the issue is the opposite: Gandhi's vision of his own purified self is the enlarged projection of a non-ideal or ideal public. This surplus self of national sovereignty can be best contained within a strict ethic of self-control, limited of course by the ethic of self-sacrifice.

In a letter to Manu, after she pledged herself to the brahmacharya experiment, Gandhi directs her: 'Keep your word. Never hide even a single thought from me. Give me the whole truth as you know it, whenever I want to know something from you. The step I took today was taken after grave deliberation. Put down in writing for me your reaction to it. I will be utterly frank with you and apprise you of all my thoughts. But all I want at present from you is this: let it be ingrained in your mind that whatever I tell you or want from you is always for your good.' After Manu's father left her behind, Gandhi instructed her to read her diary to him. She objected, saying she was 'ashamed' to read her 'confessions aloud' to him. Gandhi explained to her the 'greater purification in boldly confessing one's shortcomings face to face than by simply writing them down for others to read.'

Gandhi had once told Manu: 'I am your mother. Am I not? It is enough, if you understand this much.' Manu too had exclaimed on another occasion: 'And oh, joy!...It is I who am that beloved child of Mother Bapu!' Nirmal Kumar Bose found Gandhi's adoption as Manu's mother one of the 'rare [but] established modes of the subordination of sex among spiritual aspirants in India.' Bose goes on to say: 'It was by becoming...woman that he tried to circumvent one of the most powerful and disturbing elements which belong to our biological existence.' Gandhi's idea of brahmacharya did not mean 'not to touch a woman'. In Gandhi's description, 'brahmacharya is a thought and practice that puts you in touch with the Infinite.' His brahmacharya is an endless possibility of self-control. The quest for touching the 'Infinite' is simultaneously a quest for infinite power. The 'Infinite' of brahmacharya is the surplus of the Gandhian experiment, producing a range of activities, divided between night and day, and merging the political and spiritual.

Nirmal Kumar Bose had raised with Gandhi of Manu's silence on the brahmacharya experiment: 'I first ascertained from you if she had any connection with your experiment, and you answered in the affirmative...[She] told me sometime ago that she had nothing to do with your *prayog* that maybe she was screening facts, even from herself.' In a letter to Gandhi, Bose raised an issue regarding Gandhi's division of labour between his nightly (personal) and daytime (public) activities. Between Manu and Bose, we find two different versions of recording events in Noakhali, in the modernist spirit of the Stoic tradition, as Michel Foucault pointed out, where 'one had to record what happened every day, both the life of the day and the life of the night.' The Gandhian surplus of the self-in-politics is ultimately faced by a divided praxis: between brahmacharya, the ethic of self-control, and satyagraha, the politics of truth haunted by sacrifice.

~

Babasaheb Ambedkar enters the debate on nationalism and Hindu culture as a prime antagonist and the most uncompromising interlocutor. Born an outcaste, in the untouchable Mahad community in Maharashtra, Ambedkar struggled through humiliation from upper-caste Hindus to earn his doctorates in economics from both Columbia University and the London School of Economics. His writings on caste have gained the kind of reputation that is accorded to the best thinkers of any time in any country. But even after his death, recognition for Ambedkar in academic and public discourse in India was slow in coming. There is undoubtedly a history of great denial and discrimination behind the reluctance of so many scholars to engage with Ambedkar's formidable critique of politics, nationalism and culture.

In his famously undelivered lecture, *The Annihilation of Caste*, Ambedkar makes the radical argument against 'Indians whose patriotism does not permit them to admit that Indians are not a nation, that they are only an amorphous mass of people.' He calls Hindu society 'a myth' because the name 'Hindu' was given by Muslim invaders, showing that Hindus 'did not feel the necessity of a common name, because they had no conception of their having constituted a community.'

He disqualifies Hindu society even as a society belonging to 'people', as the term 'people' denotes a collective. Ambedkar argues that not only do Hindus not constitute a collective, but 'Hindu Society as such does not exist. It is only a collection of castes. Each caste is conscious of its existence. Its survival is the be-all and end-all of its existence. Castes do not even form a federation. A caste has no feeling that it is affiliated to other castes, except when there is a Hindu-Muslim riot. On all other occasions each caste endeavours to segregate itself and to distinguish itself from other castes.' Ambedkar denies Hindus the status of a society by attaching purely western-centric norms of what constitutes a society. What prevents Hindus from gaining the aspirational status of a society and a community is the peculiar structure of fixed, internal differentiation that is caste. Hindus, being named by others as a community, disparate may appear to be a people belonging to a common belief *from the outside*. But from *within*, the story is quite different.

Ambedkar puts Tagore's critique of the nation on a different plane. He does not critique the idea of the nation, but the false claim made by Hindus who aspire to it. From Ambedkar's perspective, we can critique the idea of India as an 'imagined community', for the idea of the nation does not emanate in the case of Hindus from any concrete historical or sociological experience of being a people, or community. Hindu society is a misnomer, signifying a concept empty from within, where only castes exist. Can there be a nation of castes? Ambedkar would say no. Though there is another disturbing aspect to the story, of castes gaining fellow-feeling only under a negative condition, involving violence against another community. The idea of unity among Hindus is predicated upon the question of survival, not a sense of community in daily life. The point is not whether we can disqualify Hindu society as a society, or its people as people. We have to engage with the deep ethical, historical and political problems in calling Hindus a community in the modern sense.

Ambedkar further elaborates, 'There is an utter lack among the Hindus of what sociologists call "consciousness of kind". There is no Hindu consciousness of kind. In every Hindu, the consciousness that exists is the consciousness of his caste. That is the reason why the Hindus cannot be said to form a society or a nation.' The point is that the idea of a nation hinges upon the pre-existing consciousness of a people, and the Hindus lack it.

One may argue that the colonial encounter did manage to instill a sense of national spirit and consciousness. Colonies were forced to become nations which had to justify themselves by imagining a certain history and consciousness of a people. It was a pedagogical and political project to legitimize nationalism. Regarding this inventive mode of recreating the past, Ernest Gellner says 'Nationalism is not the awakening of nations to self-consciousness: it invents nations where they do not exist.' This statement is a lock-stock-and-barrel fact for colonies like India. It is however not necessary to pit national self-consciousness against inventing the nation. Critiquing Gellner, Benedict Anderson makes the subtle point that it is not 'falsity or genuineness of nations that matters but *the way* in which they are imagined' (Emphasis added). Nationalist imagination is a matter of style, as much as of necessity, where political and ethical values are expected to converge but often don't. Nationalism is largely about pride and history. That sentiment may freely and unethically distort history at will to suit its pride. It corroborates Nehru's view on 'an unreliable friend and an unsafe historian.' In India's case, the tension between falsity and genuineness often reaches breaking point in hagiographies of Congress leaders by scholars. The Hindu

Right is even more brazen in letting play second fiddle to religious and community pride, fiddling with history textbooks in order to recreate the past in the Hindu nationalist self-image and denying 'outsiders' their place in Indian history.

In the matter of imagining the past, India could compete with Britain, but it still had to look for this nation in history. It is precisely at this point that Ambedkar's rejection of Hindu claims to the nation becomes interesting. But before we turn to Ambedkar, let us read Anderson on the clinching factor which helps a community imagine the nation:

> Finally, it is imagined as a community, because, regardless of the actual inequality and exploitation that may prevail in each, the nation is always conceived as a deep, horizontal comradeship. Ultimately it is this fraternity that makes it possible, over the past two centuries, for so many millions of people, not so much to kill, as willingly to die for such limited imaginings.

In *Untouchables or The Children of India's Ghetto*, Ambedkar writes, 'In this Republic, there is no place for democracy. There is no room for equality. There is no room for liberty and there is no room for fraternity. The Indian village is the very negation of a Republic. If it is a republic, it is a republic of the Touchables, by the Touchables and for the Touchables. The republic is an Empire of the Hindus over the Untouchables. It is a kind of colonialism of the Hindus designed to exploit the Untouchables.' It is evident there is no 'horizontal relationship' between Hindus and untouchables, which nullifies any fraternity. On the colonialism of the Hindus, I am reminded of Jacques Derrida's reply to a question I had asked him in JNU during his lecture in January 1997, where he spoke about his Algerian childhood. I had asked him if the history of the mother tongue was tainted by a history of power. He responded: saying that 'All cultures are *originally* colonial.'

Aishwary Kumar, in *Radical Equality*, quotes Ambedkar's statements during the Constituent Assembly debates in 1949, that 'fraternity can be a fact only when there is a nation', and that 'caste is anti-national'. Ambedkar firmly echoes Anderson's point about fraternity being a key aspect of the nation's imagined community. Caste is anti-national because it prevents fraternal relations.

Hegel was admirably alive to the question of caste in India, as he wrote in his *General Introduction to the Philosophy of History* (originally delivered as lectures at the University of Berlin in 1822, 1828 and 1830): 'In that country the impulse of organization, which begins to differentiate society, was immediately petrified into the natural distinctions of castes. The laws, thus, concern the civil rights, but make them dependent on these natural distinctions. They determine primarily mutual prerogatives of the castes—*wrongs rather than rights*—namely, of the higher against the lower. Therewith the element of morality is banished from the splendor of Indian life and its empires' (Emphasis added).

This is quite a brilliant summary of the caste problem and the question of morality. The distinction of castes based on birth creates a wedge between universal rights and rights by privilege. Hegel beautifully plays on the words 'wrongs' and 'rights' to signify what is morally wrong in the fixed relations between castes and emphasize the limited nature of civil rights within the casteist hierarchy. The universality which Tagore spoke of, whether in a determinate or higher form, is severely compromised by the rigid relations of caste, a problem Tagore blithely ignores.

In the paper 'Castes in India', presented at the 'Anthropology Seminar' in Columbia University on 9 May 1916, Ambedkar raises the question of the surplus man and woman from a perspective very different from Tagore's. Ambedkar speaks about the widow in Hindu society as the 'surplus woman', who is 'disposed of, else through intermarriage she will violate the endogamy of the group.' Ambedkar explains, 'She may marry outside the Caste and violate endogamy, or she may marry within the Caste and through competition encroach upon the chances of marriage that must be reserved for the potential brides in the Caste.' According to Ambedkar, 'Sati, enforced widowhood and girl marriage are customs that were primarily intended to solve the problem of the surplus man and surplus woman in a caste and to maintain its endogamy.' The status of the widower in Hindu society as the 'surplus man', Ambedkar finds more pernicious, and 'much more difficult than that of the surplus woman in a group that desires to make itself into a Caste'. Having 'traditional superiority' over women, and being a 'maker of injunctions', the surplus man is not forced into practising celibacy as that would affect 'the material wellbeing of his Caste'. So the best remedy for a surplus man is to be 'provided with a wife only by recruiting a bride from the ranks of those not yet marriageable in order to tie him down to the group.'

Ambedkar finds clues to the many 'origins of caste' in India in these rules and customs of endogamy. In the sphere of social practices of Hindu society, the idea of 'surplus' plays a dubious role, quite different from Tagore's idea of the surplus man as a figure of art, science and creativity. Ambedkar's surplus man and woman are not their own surplus but figures who are considered to be in surplus to the strict cultural economy of endogamy practised within the caste system. The anthropological fact of forced endogamy defines an exceptional caste norm, as a set of rules that prohibit free choices of life.

The origin of Untouchability lies buried in a dead past which nobody knows.

—B.R. Ambedkar

If India is a nation with an internal territorialization that separates people by their caste and institutes the social practice of untouchability, it is our task to comprehend how it comes into being, what led Hindus to put it in place. Ambedkar traces the history of untouchability in *The Untouchables: Who Were They? And Why They Became Untouchables*. His contention is that the 'modern' condition of untouchability is 'intimately connected with cow-killing and eating beef'. Anyone who treated the cow as profane was guilty of sin and unfit for association. This is a remarkable thesis to encounter today, when the Hindu Right is demarcating a sacred space by demonizing, killing and legally prohibiting others in the name of cow slaughter and beef eating.

Ambedkar quotes D.R. Bhandarkar on cow killing being made a capital offence by the Gupta kings around 400 A,D. The phenomenon coincides with, in Ambedkar's historical thesis, the coming of Buddhism, the 'Buddhists rejected the Brahmanic religion which consisted of Yajna and animal sacrifice, particularly of the cow.' The Brahmins' 'new-found love and reverence to the cow', Ambedkar writes, made the 'Broken Men' who continued to eat beef, 'guilty of sacrilege'. The 'Broken Men' were the *original* 'aliens', tribesmen who were considered 'Asprashya', or impure, before being eventually classified as untouchables. To confirm the 'date of birth' of untouchability during the period of the Guptas, he turns to Chinese traveller, Yuan Chwang, from 629 A.D., and settles for the beginning of the modern structure and practice of untouchability at around 400 A.D. Ambedkar finds it astonishing that, forced by the encounter with Buddhism,

Brahmins gave up beef-eating 'in spite of Manu and contrary to his directions.' This legal injunction which drew its moral sanction from elevating the cow to the status of a holy animal, found both legal and moral cause to segregate those people who did not refrain from the practice of killing cows and eating beef. Under this new law, a huge list of communities were accorded an inferior status and were eventually classified as 'untouchable'. This 'terrifying list' of 429 communities, which Ambedkar estimates to be 50–60 million people, continue today to be born into the system of 'hereditary Untouchability'. It is the most bizarre taxonomy of human beings segregated according to their occupation. Ambedkar proves two related facts: one, that there was a lack of evidence from scriptural sources, and two, that untouchability emerged as a product of historical and social reasons.

Ambedkar's concluding remarks on the modern form of untouchability emphasize it as 'a case of *territorial segregation* and of a cordon sanitaire putting the impure people inside a barbed wire into a sort of a cage' (Emphasis added). He calls the 'ghettoes' that untouchables are forced to live in 'permanent segregation camps'. As a principle and as a law of exclusion, 'territorial segregation' began with the naming of *Antya*. It is the first name, the name of an origin of untouchability, which bears the figure that is named outside the law of territory, and the territory of law. Theodore Benfey's *Sanskrit-English Dictionary* defines 'Antya' as 'Last Man...Lowest', someone of 'a very low class', a 'Chandala' and 'one of a barbarous nation'. Charles Rockwell Lanman's *A Sanskrit Reader* defines 'Antya' as 'being at the end; lowest; of lowest caste'. Ambedkar holds though that 'the word *Antya* occurs in six places (in two Sutras and four Smritis), not one enumerates who they are.' In order to solve this discrepancy, he turns to the *Manusmriti*: 'Antya as a class is mentioned in Manu

IV.79. Manu however does not enumerate them. Medhatithi in his commentary suggests that Antya means Mleccha, such as Meda etc. Bühler translates Antya as a low-caste man.' In Bühler's translation of *The Laws of Manu*, the shloka reads: 'Let him not stay together with outcasts, nor with Kandalas, nor with Pukkasas, nor with fools, nor with overbearing men, nor with low-caste men, nor with Antyavasayins [4.79].'

Antya announces a new moment, a new encounter that facilitates the need to invent a name that would fix the boundaries. This territorializing, born out of the encounter, is founded upon exclusion made possible through the naming of 'aliens' and placing them outside one's own 'quarters'. The origin is (always) the origin of an encounter, where the act of naming takes place by simultaneously naming its exclusion. There is a word, *Khôra*, which is the origin (of the name), that comes to us from Greece. It is a term that designates, Jacques Derrida writes, a 'place occupied by someone…marked place, rank, post, assigned position, territory, or region.' Derrida explores (and deconstructs) the word for both name and place. The word is comparable, from another cultural register, to Antya, which is also a name and a place for a particular subject of history, and shares a speculative historical relationship with untouchability. The echoes between Khôra and Antya suggest how the name (and the place) of origins is marked by a tacit game between *mythos* and *logos*, between story and concept, in other words, marked by *discourse*.

This act of naming fills the abyss with considerations that are proper to a discourse of politics. Unlike Khôra however, Antya names a proper subject. But it borrows the duality of Khôra that lies, as Derrida puts it, between the 'logic of exclusion and that of participation'. In Antya, this logic of exclusion and participation is written into the very dual logic of its forced adhering to a social law, which involves both exclusion and participation. In this sense, Antya prefigures the predicament of the modern Dalit subject.

The Dalit subject is both a part of Hindu society and an outsider, an 'alien'. Dalits are denied the affinity of kinship. The lack of kinship in Hindu society emanates from what Ambedkar calls in *Annihilation*, 'the separatist feeling—the feeling of being aliens—created by Caste'. This point can be extended to the point about nationalism which Ambedkar makes in *Pakistan or the Partition of India*. He finds that 'national feeling (is) a double edged feeling'. It is 'at once a feeling of fellowship for one's own kith and kin and an anti-fellowship feeling for those who are not one's own kith and kin…It is a longing *not to belong to any other group*' (Emphasis added). The Hindu idea of nationality is thus marked by an internally exclusionary structure of feeling. This is precisely how caste disturbs the sentimental discourse of nationalism.

The birth of the nation-state is a birth that intersects many histories, of which colonialism is the latest. The history of caste and modern untouchability is a part of that longer history. Its political significance was sidelined during the anticolonial struggle by both the Congress and the Left. Gail Omvedt quotes E.M.S. Namboodiripad's view on Ambedkar's demand for separate electorates in 1932, from his book, *A History of Indian Freedom Struggle*: 'This was a great blow to the freedom movement. For this led to the diversion of people's attention from the objective of full independence to the mundane cause of the upliftment of the Harijans.' Treating the question of caste and untouchability as a 'diversion' from the national cause is to differentiate and hierarchize different struggles according to the universalizing demands of nationalism.

Borrowing crudely from Marx's understanding of the history of slavery, Namboodiripad wrote in *The National Question in Kerala*, that 'the difference between one caste and another is a difference in the stage reached by them in the evolution of society'. Despite acknowledging its exploitative structure, Namboodiripad thought the caste system facilitated organized production through a systematic allocation of labour. He ignores the modern, historical phenomenon that every form of social practice (and exploitation) in India is casteist. Caste creates conditions of prejudice between the bourgeois and the working class (where the scavenging class/caste goes unnamed). This prejudice becomes part of the relations of production, as caste introduces elements of segregation and humiliation within those relations. In the case of untouchables, one might call it *relations of waste*. Those engaged in tasks like the disposal of sewage are not accorded even the minimum standard of dignified working conditions.

It was left to Ambedkar to pronounce the difference between the Marxist idea of labour and caste, in *Annihilation*: 'Caste System is not merely division of labour. *It is also a division of labourers.*' The division of labourers within a society of castes is based on a notional sense of difference instituted by the law of exclusion. It is not merely a structural division. They are divided by a law of segregation that comes *prior to* and overrides any law of mere social hierarchy, or the law of the state which promotes the equalizing law of citizenry. Among mainstream nationalist leaders within the Congress, Gandhi alone addressed that history. However, Ambedkar uncovered Gandhi's inexplicable and dubious duality, that 'though he was against untouchability he was not against caste.'

～

The difference between Ambedkar and other important thinkers of the Indian nationalist movement perhaps lies in his radical gesture towards recreating Indian/Hindu society. Having suffered discrimination, he was in no mood to compromise on matters that concerned his people. He shared Nehru's liberalism without sharing his optimism about caste disappearing in a liberal-minded society. His idea of the cultural surplus of Hindu society was critical and anthropological, rather than seeped in Tagorean metaphysics. We shall see later how he added a Buddhist twist to Gandhi's idea of nonviolence based on self-practice, by advocating a nonviolent community. It is interesting to note that Gandhi alone engaged with Ambedkar publicly. But besides their arguments, what really kept them apart was Ambedkar's indictment of Gandhi's motives. They were sailing on two different boats. On Gandhi's boat was written 'persuasion', on Ambedkar's 'resistance'. Despite being the maker of the Constitution, Ambedkar believed in the annihilation of social laws. This was perhaps what made him the most challenging figure of India's modern political history. No thinker on the Indian Left grappled with the historicity of caste, including the foundational prejudice of its origins. This made the Left's critique of social institutions partial and limiting.

On a personal note, reading all these thinkers today, I am most struck by the difference Ambedkar makes to something as fundamental as carrying (if not *being*) my name. Reading Ambedkar, I become acutely aware of his texts being unwelcoming, holding me at a distance, telling me about the law that names me and him, and by naming us, separates us. With no expectations of friendship from me, his texts transfix me as I read, pause to think, and read again, asking myself, 'How do I meet and overcome, this radical refusal of expectations?' I draw my answer from the way Derrida speaks about 'response' in *On the Name*, as 'responsibility', as 'debt', as 'duty', as something you owe yourself as much as you owe the other. Ambedkar's texts, even in their turning away from me, in their discarding any affective and ethical expectations, nevertheless ask me to respond. No text which is not a text of law, which does not question the law and place itself outside its territorial apathy, will seek a response. How not to respond to a text that moves you, if you claim that it does? It is to the force of this question, to the force of the act that provokes the question, the act of discarding and renaming, for the sake of a new fraternity, that I shall submit with no one's permission, and with whatever grace I have at my disposal.

2

Territory without Justice

The nation is born, on the one side, with the promise of freedom, generosity, dignity, and above all, justice. While on the other, it is marked by a date where the long shadow of Partition falls over the flying doves celebrating independence. Since then, the stories of betrayal, hatred, and above all, the fetish for territory, haven't come to an end. This chapter analyzes the fate and predicament of the nation's most beleaguered people—the refugees, the Dalits and the minorities—from 1947 till today.

≈

Before you ask for justice–make sure that you won't get it, just by accident.

—Paavo Haavikko,
Fifteen Epigrams in Praise of the Tyrant

Nations are born with, and live by, dates. But are dates the most promising reminders of freedom? Dates are promising only because they promise people a freedom that wasn't available to them before. In other words, dates are promising only because they announce a certain beginning towards the promise of freedom. If those freedoms have not been realized in people's lives, if the promises haven't been granted, then those dates, too, lose meaning. Dates can't simply be relics we hold on to for sentimental comfort, for jingoistic pride, unless they have kept their promise to the future. Every date is meaningful, not only vis-à-vis our past but also our future. If Independence Day marks a new beginning in the fate and life of a people who were under British colonialism, it also marks a day when the Indian nation promised its people a host of things that freedom brings. If dates promise a break with an un-free past, they are also bound to grant people the freedom they are looking for in the future. If today we have to assess the meaning of a date, it can't simply be a cyclical commemoration of what it meant to people in the beginning, but a reckoning of whether that date has kept its promise to the future. Dates are mere accidents which cannot exhaust the future of freedom.

In his speech during the series of open-air lectures on nationalism held in Jawaharlal Nehru University in early 2016, Gopal Guru, professor of political science, said 'the nation has to be imagined...in terms of the promises the nation is making.' These, clearly, are promises that the nation is making to its present and its future. What Guru calls the promise of the nation resonates in Jacques Derrida's idea of 'democracy to come'. The promise of a nation is nothing but a promise of democracy. Derrida speaks of a 'democracy that must have the structure of a promise.' 'The idea of a promise,' he writes, 'is inscribed in the idea of a democracy: equality, freedom, freedom of speech, freedom of the press.' These are then the concrete forms of the structure and spirit of democracy where, for Derrida, a future can be imagined. He calls it both a historical and political set of concepts which are deeply linked to the fundamental idea of what comprises a democracy.

Coming from the historical and political tradition of Ambedkar's thought, Guru may also like to add the idea of a new fraternity, a fraternity of the not-yet nation, of the not-yet democracy to come. Derrida, like Ambedkar, emphasizes fraternity as a key element in a just polity. He proposes in *Politics of Friendship*, that 'there is no democracy without the "community of friends".' Meditating on the question of fraternity, Derrida writes: 'Truth, freedom, necessity, and equality come together in this politics of fraternity.' Ambedkar knew caste was antithetical to the idea of fraternity, and perhaps because of that very reason, presages Derrida's point in these exact words: 'Where there is equality, there is fraternity and where there is fraternity, there is truth. And any action to establish these principles is Satyagraha!' However, the problem of memory remains.

Memory divides and creates enemies, unless reconciled by the necessity of a fraternal future. Fraternity is never natural; it is always political. Whether under secular garbs or spiritual sanctions, fraternity in a democracy is best declared and kept open. The 'sovereign friendship of secrecy', Derrida points out, is only possible between two. The 'brotherhood... of political secrecy' begins with three. Lenin, in his 1902 pamphlet *What Is to Be Done?*, calls for such a communist brotherhood of 'strict secrecy' as a 'necessary condition' for any political organization. Lenin was thinking about the Party, not fraternity. The Iron Curtain was a travesty of the idea of communism. Gandhi's politics of truth was fiercely contrary. Politics, for Gandhi, meant public confession (and discussion) of all activities, including the private. Tridip Suhrud, explaining Gandhi's method, writes: 'An experiment with Truth cannot have any possibility of secrecy.' Gandhi laid a lot of emphasis on friendship between communities, and perhaps that was why he preferred openness rather than secrecy. Friendship, for Gandhi, was the only desirable means towards justice. In *Philosophy of Hinduism*, Ambedkar said that 'justice is simply another name for liberty, equality, and fraternity.' There is surely a common echo here between Ambedkar and Gandhi. Even though they had differences regarding the two key words, 'fraternity' and 'justice', what is crucial is their connecting the idea of justice with fraternity.

The word, the concept, the demand, which haunts the claims of any nation, is justice. It is through the measure of justice alone that we may measure the promise of a nation. Can a nation be just? How do we measure a just nation? A nation is considered just by the promise of justice it grants its people. I say 'people' and not citizens, for the nation is ethically bound to help even those it considers non-citizens, i.e. migrants and refugees who are caught in territorial demarcations which violate the human rights to land and livelihood. How is justice given? Not simply by laws and court verdicts, though these are a fundamental part of the system of justice. Apart from the justice system, there is also the promise that lies in allowing people freedom—freedom to speak, think, criticize and break the strangleholds of prejudice, freedom to speak against violence and to remind people of the promise of justice. If this freedom is denied to the people, the nation is not only going against its ethical duty, it is destroying its promise. Freedom and justice are thickly entwined with each other.

Under ideal conditions, those who aren't suffering the plight of the migrant or the refugee raise their voice in solidarity. If the nation is not promising for some, it can't be promising for all. But the nation's most pampered and privileged are reluctant and indifferent when it comes to issues other than inflation, corruption or law and order. They are not interested in matters which affect the underprivileged sections of society. This social division is not merely the doing of a nation, but a proliferation of historical and social differences, which the nation acknowledges but does not erase. The constitution has the limited promise of safeguarding our rights and directing the state to grant special rights to the underprivileged. A larger sense of promise lies with the people themselves, for they alone can voice what they lack and suffer. A promise, paradoxically, comes from lack. The privileged, attached to the self-serving structures of cultural and economic ownership, lack the promise born out of lack. Democracy lives in the promise of people overcoming their privileges and attending to other people. But such a spirit rarely manages to stir the utilitarian lethargy (and logic) of the privileged. A promise is not something external, something that reduces people to passive receptors, much like what the political parties offer as gift packages during elections. A promise is something more sacred and liberating.

The country's liberation from colonial rule has not delivered the many freedoms people are still fighting for today. It only ensured a promise, made by the nation to its people, of the freedom to come. For Thomas Hobbes and David Hume, freedom meant the absence of external obstructions. This is what Isiah Berlin later termed in his lecture *Two Concepts of Liberty* (1958) as 'negative liberty'. By 'positive liberty', Berlin meant the freedom to act or decide without threats and compulsions. In his essay *On The Jewish Question* (1843), Marx had already combined these two ideas. He described liberty as the realization of human potentiality. But this potentiality, for Marx, was best served in relational terms, one that led towards an emancipatory community.

The reservation policy in India may serve as a good example to bring together these ideas of liberty. Dalits and other backward castes want reservations to be able to minimize the social prejudices against them and reach the level of confidence and mobility enjoyed by the privileged castes. But this liberty is not enough for the 'positive liberty' they seek, which is the capability to assert their political and cultural aspirations. Both liberties work, in different ways, to ensure two different modes of capability and ways of being free. It is the combination of both which forms the background for Ambedkar's idea of 'social justice'. For Ambedkar, the Hindu religion fails the 'test of justice' from the point of view of the untouchables, as it fails to offer them freedom. The same question may be asked of the nation: Has the nation ensured Dalits the freedom it ensures others? There is no justice without freedom. Can there be freedom without justice?

In the provocative lines of this chapter's epigraph, which accident of justice is the Finnish poet and aphorist, Paavo Haavikko, warning us against? We may consider the date of liberation from colonial rule an accident that had serious consequences. It was motivated by various historical and political factors that gifted us freedom and Partition in one stroke. The 'stroke of the midnight hour', which Nehru eulogized, was also the midnight of horror for many. The vultures preying over dead bodies in Bengal and Punjab offered a stark contrast to the doves flying from the Red Fort. When a date is reason for both jubilation and grief, can such a date simply define freedom? How can the birth of the nation be just if Partition was unjust? It isn't about how we look at freedom and justice as mere ideas to be debated, but the actual cost of lives that pose limits to those ideas. Ideas cannot be free from the question of death—in this context, the deaths that followed independence and the Partition. Neither the British nor the Congress claimed sincere responsibility for the countless lives lost during the birth of the nation. It was a date they decided together, without anticipating the consequences. One accident often triggers another.

The Greek term *hamartia*, discussed by Aristotle in *Poetics*, covers a broad spectrum of meanings, including ignorance, error or accidental wrongdoing. Though based on the frailties of human character, we may reasonably extend it to talk about a community or 'national character'. What if the nation's character is constitutively flawed, accidental, beginning with its madness for dates and the shortcomings of justice?

To say that independence/Partition produced our moment of *hamartia* would be to acknowledge a congenital flaw in the nation's character. Perhaps the worst proof of this lies in the fact that Partition enhanced and hardened communal prejudices. This flaw remains ignored and unacknowledged by another trait of national character for which also originates in Greece: *hubris*, or foolish and dangerous self-pride. The communal nature of the Assam Movement is a good example. Such sub-national movements fall into the trap of communalizing society, where the original sin of the nation (i.e. Partition) is replicated in the name of securing the demands (economic, social and political) of a territorially determined linguistic majority. India is a country of not only religious but also linguistic minorities, spread across its many states. To harass these minorities in the name of identitarian aspirations of any majority community is undemocratic. Political campaigns based on language and ethnicity will have to draw an ethical line between ambition and fraternal reconciliation.

~

Forward? We've tried that before:
Why not regress, quickly
And without stopovers?

—Günter Grass, *What We Lack*

It is easier to be united in outrage against a singular, spectacularly brutal act of violence than against the normalized, everyday violence of the state anywhere in the world. The latter not only creates much less outrage than it should, but is often justified in the name of territorial morality. So everyone may unite against the terrorist attack in France, but opinions are divided when people talk, for instance, about Kashmir. Here people find space for taking sides. Though what connects both cases is the question of national boundaries, where all our values seem to rest and cancel out everything else. But hope today has strict borders. Beyond these borders, hope does not exist. Hope is a territorialized beast roaming inside a nation's nightmares.

Walter Benjamin writes in his famous *Theses on the Philosophy of History*, 'There is no document of civilization which is not at the same time a document of barbarism.' Scratch the surface of a civilization and you will find petty historical sentiments and passions lurking, ready to pounce on you if you fiddle too much with them. Modernity has contributed to inventing the fiction of nations. Nations are fictions (social, political, historical) in the name of a larger community, bound by what Benedict Anderson called 'print capitalism' and collective memory, among other cultural factors. Examine the individuals belonging to this so-called community and you will discover regional and religious sentiments spewing venom. The native today is as aggrieved and angry as the migrant. There are instances of natives being forced to become migrants in their own country by the devious machinations of particular communities playing territorial politics.

Political disputes around the question of territory still lack good grounds for reconcilement. The native and the migrant (or the majority and the minority, or even two linguistic or religious communities belonging to the same place) rarely share the same values. The citizen—that privileged subject of liberal democracies—cannot therefore claim a superior status against those it declares non-citizens (migrants, refugees).

The edifice of modernity rests on moral and political ideas professed by the Enlightenment. These ideas or values are ratified by the Universal Declaration of Human Rights. But they don't solve old hostilities, even as they create new ones which involve radical cultural differences or historically embedded social hierarchies (taking new forms). The other, ignored in the political history of every civilization, has lost its temper and is looking for revenge. The other is out to sever ties, to erase the self that created it.

~

> *Words that behaved and carried meaning*
> *Have turned their coats.*
> —Günter Grass, *Dreaming Ahead*

The rationalized myths of modernity are giving way. Modernity fictionalized our identities. We shared certain universal codes (and norms) of aesthetics and politics, holding shared values with others despite our differences. That shared bit is now under question, if not already rejected. No one is willing to share anything with anyone anymore. Salman Rushdie's phrase, 'translated men', describes our innovative cultural selves perfectly. Not any longer. Today it sounds like a beautiful but feeble attempt to gloss over people's fundamentalist or racist predispositions. There is currently a refusal of the migrant and hybrid self which Rushdie championed in his novels. There is a growing myopia against the translatability of identity, of 'bearing across' the borders in order to embrace the other side, a phenomenon that inspired people throughout our history, from Dara Shikoh to Raghupati Sahay (better known as Firaq Gorakhpuri). A fascist campaign has managed to convince people that anything that does not divide is a lie. It exposes a psyche and logic of war: in history, only hate is real; the rest is conspiracy. The politics of revenge carries a notebook of historical grievances.

Since none of the problems which modernity threw up

were getting solved or addressed honestly, various sorts of anti-modernists have concluded that the best solution is to throw the baby out with the bathwater—reject modern norms and create your own, older world of logic, power and community. Modernity is evil for those who seek the luxuries of old hierarchies, prejudices and repressions. Of course, they indulge in the pleasures which capitalism and other lures of modern life bring to their doorstep. But their hypocrisy allows these 'necessities' and rejects the values which make them possible. Anti-modernists are the split-children of modernity, part denial and part harangue.

When we say those who kill in the name of religion are simply perverts who misuse the good name of religion, we push the real question of violence to the sphere of interpretation alone. Religious beliefs have sanctioned war and misogyny throughout history. Similarly, those who commit violence in the name of the nation are not simply those who interpret the nation incorrectly. They also prove, as Tagore so clearly saw, the real and violent possibility written into the very idea of the nation. Buddhism is perhaps the only religion whose origins are nonviolent. But violence has been integral to the historical march of all religions. There are, however, shining instances in earlier eras of the other being accorded pride of place in a religious culture, and invited into deep scholastic and spiritual engagement.

In the stone pillars of Hampi, one finds Turkish musicians carved beside Hindu divinities. This corroborates the 'astonishing inclusive capacity' of ancient Indian culture, which Nehru eulogized in *The Discovery of India*. In Hampi's famous stone chariot, one finds carvings of Chinese, Mongolian and Persian travellers. This shows the other history—the history which, despite the history of war, was eloquently represented as part of one's own civilization.

Today, a visit by a Sufi singer from across the border is cause for tension. The West invented national borders, both for itself and the people it colonized. These borders, even as they are virulently emphasized in majoritarian terms, have fallen apart economically. A good example is of the two Germanys, East and West, sorting out not only the currency blues of the East but also their politically enforced divide through a historic rapprochement, and breaking the Wall.

In *One Earth, Four or Five Worlds*, Octavio Paz said, in the context of the late Ayatollah Khomeini, that modernity must learn to speak to its other, through a 'buried language', which is at once archaic and modern. It is, according to Paz, the 'language of a resurrection', which modernity represses but cannot wish away. The buried language of (religious) resurrection persists beneath the secular veneer of modernity. Terrorism violently parodies this language and has to be seen as a bizarre symptom responding to modernity's crimes. It cannot be rejected, wished away or contained by security webs alone, as repeated acts of terror prove. Modernity has been brutalizing old historical relations beyond redemption.

To reclaim the lively relationship with the other in the midst of deep animosities, we may need to remember what Benjamin said in *One Way Street*: 'The only way of knowing a person is to love them without hope.' Benjamin offers a liberating option by, firstly, privileging love over knowledge as the only desirable form of knowing the other, and secondly, by freeing the anxiety of hope from any calculable expectations. To love without hope is the only way both love and hope can be tested, and their possibilities realized.

~

Speaking about immigrants to *The New York Times* in May 2016, the late Polish sociologist and philosopher Zygmunt

Bauman was reminded of a phrase of Bertolt Brecht's, 'harbingers of bad news.' He meant to say that immigrants 'embody' a certain fear and anxiety in privileged inhabitants of a place, of losing their economic, cultural and political status in the world. Refugees or migrants, Bauman explained, bring with them a certain insecurity regarding mysterious and obscure 'global forces' which disturb the stable idea of a neighbourhood. Hence the world resents dispossessed people, who are demonized, ironically, for what they do not possess. The safety of populations, ensured by their status as citizens in nation-states, lulls them into thinking of territory as sacrosanct. Refugees are seen as a threat to territory, and by logical extension, to the idea of a secure life. The heightened idea of security which runs the world today, paradoxically, only manages to heighten people's paranoia of insecurity. Today nations do not only live with the military threat of a powerful enemy across their borders. Their paranoia extends towards dispossessed people *within* their own borders, people who are seen as encroachers upon their land.

It may be tempting to relate this intensification of fear of refugees, to a primordial condition. The political nature of this condition comes from imagining the nation as a fortress of self-preservation, its rules clearly defining who its beneficiaries should be. Though America is a nation of immigrants with enough laws to protect their interests, the sentiment of self-preservation mixed with a racist discourse of hatred towards immigrants can twist and turn those laws to pacify itself. Donald Trump's coming to power has facilitated the unleashing of this very phenomenon. In India, the deliberate lack of a clear policy and ethical responsibility towards people forced to become refugees by Partition, has kept their fate forever tottering under the sword of Damocles.

Democracy is, by definition, the antithesis of fascism. But

despite being the guarantor of formal equality and rule of law, the political idea of democracy is still subject to nationalist passions. These passions legitimize political inequality by openly coercing minorities and spreading lies about them. Racist movements exploit the tensions between democracy and nationalism, and use the crisis to their advantage. There is an unresolved hatred against the hybrid culture of modernity in all revivalist movements invested in puritanical cultural nationalism. It is not mere hypocrisy which foments the passions of a revivalist, but the manifestation of a loss they cannot come to grips with. The loss of identity is seen not in profound but monstrous terms. And the other is blamed for this crisis. These revivalisms affect the status and fate of refugees or migrants most adversely. These are people who have failed to find justice within the laws of the nation-state.

Growing up in Assam in the late 1970s and '80s, I was witness to a communal movement which massacred my idea of home. Aimed at driving out people dubiously named 'foreign nationals', it was a middle-class movement which gained popularity between late 1979 and 1984. Young students and male agitators spearheading it openly espoused and committed violence against minorities. As a refugee family from erstwhile East Bengal, we were also identified as 'foreigners' by the leaders of the Assam Movement. They displayed great virtue in thrusting the vocabulary of colonial occupation upon a beleaguered people looking for a place to begin life anew. Some of these migrants, belonging to the propertied class in East Bengal, gained government jobs in the railways and elsewhere with little education. Their social and economic status ensured a degree of safety when the anti-foreigners movement began in violent earnestness. Yet, they were seen with equal hatred, as encroachers upon a place they did not belong to. I grew up listening to stories of erstwhile East Bengal, and wondering about our relation to India. To know as a young boy one is a 'foreigner' in his own birthplace can be catastrophic. It not only severed my ties with the only place I could call home, but also put into question the relationships between land and people, people and territory, territory and language, language and belonging.

Torchlight processions would pass by our homes, chanting slogans in Assamese, 'Will give blood, not country' and 'Foreigners get out', etc. A blackout would be declared in the evening whenever a procession was planned. We had to watch them go by through dark windows of fear. Whole neighbourhoods were infected by this communal sentiment. On one occasion, a roguish teenager, with help from his mother, murdered his childhood friend in my neighbourhood. For six years, life was disrupted by threats, roadside violence, murders and stone-throwing at people reporting for work during bandhs. The word 'curfew' spread like the news of a prowling wolf. We often left a game of football midway to rush home. We were uncomfortably used to the idea of being protected by the police, as their presence reminded us we weren't free. All India Radio censored news with the logic of 'not aggravating the situation'. Imagine the precariousness of our status and our sense of trust in the nation, as every evening we had to tune in to the Bengali radio service of the BBC and Voice of America to know the fate of people belonging to our community in other parts of the state. We felt like the harbingers of bad news, not only for the local community, but also for the nation at large. The government sent us reassurances in the shape of the Central Police Force only when things got out of hand. We were out of place and out of favour.

In his essay, '"Tongue Has No Bone": Fixing the Assamese Language, c.1800–c.1930', Boddhisatva Kar provided interesting facts about the construction of Assamese grammar and language so that the British might recognize Assamese as a distinct linguistic and cultural identity. The influences of Assamese on other languages, including Bengali, were denied or explained away as spurious. This linguistic manoeuvring invented and claimed an identity which would be truer to politics than to history. All this politics came about because the local inhabitants of Assam resented the hegemony of Bengali, which was the official language of the state. Moreover the Bengali community, exposed early on to the English language, had quickly gained expertise in running a clerical bureaucracy. This served British interests as much as it helped the Bengalis gain public sector jobs.

These privileges became cause for the backlash in Assam. The communal nature of the Assam Agitation, with slogans like 'Foreigners Get Out', took the constraints of the situation to its reactionary extreme. The tongue has no bone, and yet it can spell borders, mark territories, and make hard propositions. Can the tongue be trusted? Does speech know its history? The search for origins has been one of the most dubious obsessions of modernity.

There was a Life Insurance Company office building at the entrance of the sprawling market area in Guwahati, which I used to pass by every time I visited my grandmother's place. Its board read, 'Insure and be secure'. Bengali refugees had no insurance for their political status and were left to face the communally charged music in deep insecurity. The strange knowledge of being a 'foreigner', experiencing liquid hate in the streets, under skies one thought were one's own, can forever disrupt the idea of belonging. But the desperation to be part of the national mainstream, and having enough avenues to do so, made the Bengali Hindu middle-class in Assam settle down to an apolitical existence after the Assam Accord was signed in 1985.

The Nellie riots on 18 February 1983 which preceded the accord, where thousands of Muslim peasants were butchered in a few hours, and the gradual easing off of tensions between the Bengali and the Assamese middle-class Hindus, ensured that Muslims alone would be relegated to the status of permanent, political refugees in the state. This perfectly suited the 'acceptable' communal divide in the nation. Bengali Hindus, who had faced persecution till that day, had no qualms in abandoning the Muslims to their lone political fate. Refugees who fail to grow a sense of solidarity and empathy for less fortunate others are selfish and disappointing victims of history. The lure of communal nationalism and the logic of economic profit have enough power to divide victims.

Any upsurge of cultural revivalism based on religion, language or race is bad news for the harbingers of bad news, as refugees are perceived as 'natural' outsiders within the territorial conception of the nation-state. One of the trickiest features of modern democracies is the fusion of the sacral and the natural. The reading of the Bible during the recent inauguration ceremony of the American President guts the secular idea of democracy with religious nationalism. Religious nationalism sanctifies the idea of territory in sacral terms.

Donald Trump's evocation of 'forgotten people' was clearly not meant for the neglected working-class or for marginalized minorities. By naming White Christians as the 'forgotten people', all those who fell outside this scriptural sanction became potential targets. Migrants and refugees became 'natural' outsiders. As they fall outside the sacral idea of the nation, they are seen as less than human, and more animal- or insect-like. The majority community suffers from narcissism wherein the other falls outside the discourse of love, and is therefore considered ripe for hatred.

In a scene from Werner Herzog's satirical film, *The*

Unprecedented Defence of the Fortress Deutschkreuz, a young man wearing a World War II army uniform maniacally chases a rat with a defunct gun. Hate is not just serious business, it is a game. It is fun to scare away the insect who enters our territory by accident or fate. Treating others like insects adds a special charm to being a fascist.

Brad Evans, in his interview of Bauman, quoted the British-Somalian poet Warsan Shire's famous poem on refugees: 'no one puts their children in a boat/unless the water is safer than the land.' For a refugee, the trials of land are as slippery and treacherous as water. The central problem of refugees and migrants is perhaps the articulation of a language of seeking shelter, without compromising their sense of dignity. But their dignity slips away the moment they enter someone else's territory, in a world where the very idea of the 'human' is marked by territorial sanctity.

The language of human rights works under the inherent assumptions of a secular democratic worldview and value-system. It may sensitize the state and its people to the ethical responsibility of accommodating migrants into their world, but falls short of addressing the fundamental problem: the logic of territorialized humanity, where the birth of the privileged citizen has meant the death of the migrant or the refugee. The human being as a territorialized animal seeking self-preservation needs to welcome the refugee in order to retain any possibility of their becoming human.

3

Looking for the Muslim

This chapter looks at India's Muslims, the shadow of Partition behind them, and the long shadow of the future ahead of them. The Muslims are a partitioned people within India, looking for their place in the nation's history. The history and memory of Indian nationalism provides several instances of Hindus and Muslims challenging British colonialism together. But the birth of the Hindu Right in 1925, and subsequently, ideas advocated by the Muslim League from the 1930s, came to imagine the nation in religious terms. This led to the Partition, and evident markers of a shared culture, the everyday life of friendship and neighbourhood, and imagining a secular political future, were shaken to the roots. The discourse of trust and mutual generosity was taken over by suspicion and hatred. Religion and history were treated as contested territories of difference. It led to the sacrifice of the ethical responsibility which exceeds the demands of mere identity.

~

In the aftermath of 9/11, Mahmood Mamdani has noted how the western world, headed by American politics, created a discourse that tended to distinguish between 'good Muslims' and 'bad Muslims'. There was an added inference that Islam needed to be quarantined from the influence of the latter. Mamdani emphasized the blindness in overlooking the internally diverse nature and dynamism of Islamic culture, and fixing Muslims as habitually medieval, and not at home in modernity. Such a view, Mamdani persuasively argues, collapses culture into politics, and politics into the American-aided fundamentalisms emerging from the Islamic world. I find a certain resonance of this debate in the Indian context, where competing notions of a 'good' Hindu and a 'bad' Hindu have existed since the time of the nationalist struggle. This debate took various political forms, with the cultural identity of a 'Hindu' being understood either in territorial/national or universal terms, and questioned whether being 'Hindu' in the modern world meant holding on to older texts, beliefs and practices, or ethically (and politically) remaking one's identity. It reached a high point—or low, depending on one's perspective—during Partition, but was forced to take a back seat during the 'secular' Nehruvian era. Since the latter part of the twentieth century and the dawn of the twenty-first century, however, as the Congress regime toyed with religious sentiments and the Hindu Right began to make successful bids for political power, the 'good' Hindu versus 'bad' Hindu debate has taken a decisive and dangerous political turn.

It was Gandhi who had clarified to Millie Graham Polak, 'to be a good Hindu meant I would also be a good Christian'. Elsewhere he also said, 'I am a good Hindu so I am a good Muslim.' For Gandhi, the question of being Hindu is clearly defined in ethical terms and is not exclusive of values that a good Hindu shares with a good Muslim or a good Christian. However, in his reply to Gandhi's critical response to *The Annihilation of Caste*, Ambedkar challenged Gandhi's idea of the 'good Hindu' with scathing rhetoric: '...there can be a better or a worse Hindu. But a good Hindu there cannot be.' In the context of the caste system, Ambedkar reduced the political and ethical status of the Hindu to one who practises slavery against the untouchables. He clarified, 'To a slave, his master may be better or worse. But there cannot be a good master.' This challenge to Gandhi's idea opens another serious dimension to the debate, but it does not foreclose the possibilities of ethically defining a 'good Hindu' in contexts where Hindus share a historical and political relationship with others. A good Hindu, from a Gandhian perspective, is someone who can summon cultural and ethical resources that enable an ethical relationship with others. Gandhi's quest for truth was a means to find this point of convergence, where justice between communities was possible. For Gandhi, religion was capable of ethically addressing historical and political problems.

For Veer Savarkar, on the other hand, the issue was 'What is a Hindu?' This question was tackled in terms of a genealogy going back to the concept of the 'Aryans', a sacred sense of territoriality, and a historical identity where the Hindu is one who is *not* the other he confronts—namely, outsiders like Muslims, Christians, etc. In a complete departure from Gandhi's interest in defining the *ethical* Hindu, Savarkar is interested in defining the *authentic* Hindu, a dubious project of pure roots.

Nehru, and with him, all liberal and Left ideologues, upheld the distinction between a secular and a religious Hindu or Muslim—where 'secular' replaced good and 'religious' certainly stood for bad. The religious Hindu or Muslim was seen as an anathema by the secularists and a legitimate reason for not allowing religious communities to gain political attention. But the 'good' Hindu or Muslim believer fell outside the Nehruvian secular ideal. In *The Intimate Enemy*, Ashis Nandy critiques Nehru's binary, and argues in favour of the 'sophisticated ethical sensitivity' of the Gandhian subject, who belonged to 'the other West'.

However, a further complication arose between the two. The

Nehruvian secularists were upholders of the minority-majority framework, where the secular state's role was seen not only as a neutral one, but also as a protector of minority interests and aspirations. In this, the Nehruvian secular state made a tacit demand on both majority and minority communities. Nehru writes, 'We call our state a secular one…What exactly does it mean? It does obviously mean a state where religion as such is discouraged.'

This is a liberal premise of the protectionist state. Nehru further says, 'It means that minority communities, from the religious point of view, should accept this position.' The majority 'should fully realize it' and being 'the dominant community [it owes] its responsibility not to use its position in any way which might prejudice our secular ideal.' The minorities are asked to support secularism for their own interest (to secure their private sphere) and the majority is expected to play a responsible role in guiding the secular principle.

In this demanding idea of secularism, Nehru leaves out a *political* link between the responsible role of the community and the ideology of the state, making both the spheres suspicious of each other. Akeel Bilgrami quite rightly finds Nehru's neutrality-based statist approach 'an imposition rather in the sense that it assumed that secularism stood outside the substantive arena of political commitments.' He critiques Nehru, not for his secular approach, but for 'imposing a non-negotiated secularism'. Negotiation would involve the political participation of religious communities regarding issues that matter to them. The Nehruvian state preferred to deny communities that participation.

In the introduction to his famous work, *Formations of the Secular: Christianity, Islam, Modernity*, Talal Asad sharply articulated the secular problem in India: 'A secular State does not guarantee toleration; it puts into play different structures of ambition and fear. The law never seeks to eliminate violence since its objective is always to *regulate* violence.'

The competitive economic logic of the modern nation-state makes hostility, rather than affective values like toleration, thrive between communities. When disputes arise, the government in power is prone to taking decisions that suit its political interest. The supposed neutrality of the state gets exposed as a garb for majoritarian hegemony. If state values are compromised, communities cannot remain unaffected. Instead of eliminating violence, a fascist takeover may take up the job of eliminating minorities. The contradictions of the Nehruvian secular state, being principally neutral but politically suspect, have failed to tackle majoritarianism and nurture a sense of confidence in the minorities.

Long after Nehru, during the regimes of Rajiv Gandhi and Narasimha Rao, the deliberate mishandling of the Shah Bano case and the improper management of the Babri Masjid dispute found the secular state terribly wanting in imparting justice based on its stated principles. Clearly, the principle of secular neutrality did not work. Rather, it was compromised on crucial matters when religious issues got mixed up with political stakes. Asghar Ali Engineer raises the question, 'If Golwalkar wanted people to be good Muslim and good Hindu, why was the Babri Masjid demolished? Was it being a good Hindu?' Engineer invokes a distinction similar to Gandhi's, to demand an ethical notion of being Hindu and Muslim.

With the BJP coming to power with a clear majority in 2014, the ideological shifts in the political landscape have swiftly impacted India's cultural landscape as well. The 'secular' and 'religious' distinction between the Hindu and the Muslim still exists, but the powers are reversed: today, the resurgent spirit of the 'religious' Hindu dominates the political space against secularists who are at the receiving end of threats, bans and violence. A bizarre logic is in place: the Hindu Right's investment in the 'authentic' Hindu seems to have now coopted Gandhi's ethical idea of the 'good' Hindu by creating a devious political understanding of who is a good Hindu (or Muslim), and who—by extension—is a bad Hindu or Muslim.

The good Hindu, in the Hindu Right's view today, whether secular or religious, is one who serves the larger cause of nationalism, while the bad Hindu, secular *or* religious, works against nationalist (including jingoistic) interests. The Nehruvian distinction between the secular and the religious holds no water in this neo-Hindu-Right scheme of things. It doesn't matter to the Hindu Right whether the slain writers and activists, M.M. Kalburgi, Govind Pansare and Narendra Dabholkar, were secular or religious, rationalist or irrationalist. Their internal belief system is not an issue, till it poses a threat to the Hindu Right's own belief system. The Hindu Right can be equally secular or religious, rational or irrational. But what is sacrosanct is the sentiment of nationalism.

This is a radical departure from the Gandhian subject of the ethical believer—the 'good' Hindu and Muslim—rather than the Nehruvian distinction between the 'secular' and the 'religious', or even the 'rationalist' and the 'irrationalist'. These modern distinctions don't explain the complexity of communal nationalism.

Gandhi, by all means a religious Hindu, was seen as more harmful to the Hindu political cause than a secular Nehru. In Gandhi's case, it was his reconciliatory gestures towards Muslims that earned the ire of the Hindu Right. Nathuram Godse, who killed him, claimed in court that his intentions were secular and provided strictly rational reasons in his defence for killing Gandhi. The deeper problem is not whether Godse's claim to be secular is convincing, but how the secular and the religious can be fused together in the interests of the larger value called nationalism. It must be noted in this regard that Godse, in his famous defence, accused Nehru of helping the formation of Pakistan, yet he didn't criticize Nehru for being secular. Godse felt Nehru displayed double standards by believing in secularism and yet allowing a theocratic state like Pakistan to come into being. Yet crucially, for Godse, the real enemy was Gandhi, not Nehru.

The Hindu Right today doesn't seem to straightforwardly divide Hindus and Muslims, but rather distinguishes good Hindus and Muslims from bad Hindus and Muslims. For the Hindu Right, the late president, A.P.J. Abdul Kalam, was a good Muslim, as he fashioned himself purely as a secular nationalist, involved in matters of science rather than religion. In contrast, the writer U.R. Ananthamurthy exemplified a bad Hindu, for speaking up against the caste system and Hindu nationalism. He became an undesirable literary icon. The return of the distinction between the good and the bad Hindu (or Muslim) disregards all ethical criteria, religious or secular. A Hindu is deemed 'good' in purely nationalist terms, even if she espouses hatred of minorities. A Muslim, on the other hand, is 'bad' if she asserts her political rights or sensibilities (religious or secular) as a point of difference from the Hindu majoritarian idea of the nation.

Nationalism demands commitment and submission, not ethics. Even if the bad Hindu has ethical intentions in his criticisms and objections—such as the fight against superstition, prejudice and blind belief—he is an unwanted threat to the cause of religious nationalism. The bad Hindu, ironically, has to abandon her ethical principles in the service of her nation, to gain the status of a good Hindu under the new political dispensation. The tacit assumption is there is nothing particularly secular or religious about it. The demand is, nevertheless, absolutely political: the good Hindu is one who upholds nationalism over ethics and the bad Hindu is one who upholds ethics over nationalism.

It is easier to play the game between majority and minority by relinquishing those terms and reconfiguring them into the discourse of good and bad. Gandhi tries to address the problem of good and bad by privileging criticism and fraternal feelings over blind faith and animosity. Gandhian politics was involved in finding means to minimize fear and mistrust between Hindus and Muslims through the sharing of power with the Muslim League. Nehru's approach sidelined Gandhian politics by accepting Partition because it refused to share power in the name of secular politics. The avowed neutrality of Nehru's secular state could not overcome its contradictions. Its failure has exposed us to the original problem it sidelined. The good Hindu, be it of the Gandhian or Nehruvian variety, is today the bad Hindu who is under threat. This is history returning as tragic farce.

~

Law is not justice.
—Jacques Derrida

Justice has to demonstrate a measure of equivalence. Any nation will need a sincere amount of fairness to render justice to minorities. The state has to infuse trust in them. Justice has the responsibility to heal, besides declaring punishments. Derrida spoke of the 'responsibility of memory' in relation to justice. Our nation's memory still languishes in paranoia and suspicion since Partition. That memory itself needs healing. The demolition of the Babri Masjid in December 1992 radicalized sections of Muslim youth who were to become the foot soldiers of violent agendas. And then, the Bombay riots—masterminded by Hindu groups in the triumphant aftermath of the demolition—were followed by a Pakistan-backed, Muslim-mafia-financed series of bombings in Bombay in the spring of 1993. Finally, the devastating anti-Muslim pogrom in Gujarat ten years later led to a fresh communalization of relations, predominantly in urban areas.

It was first argued by Ashis Nandy, among others, that Hindu communalism is an urban phenomenon, springing from what he called the 'urban-industrial vision' with a 'violence...hidden in its belly.' The socio-economic competition for prosperity and supremacy in urban areas led to riots and Muslims faced the most terrible reverses. But beneath the socio-political phenomena backed by ruthless economic logic, lies the older historical animosity leading back to Partition. The communal stories of Partition are one-sided and manipulative narratives, aimed at provoking and reaffirming communal sentiments.

It will be instructive to recall in this regard the second Partition of Bengal. The maverick historian Nirad C. Chaudhuri, in *Thy Hand, Great Anarch!* laid bare the technical details of how Hindu legislators in the Bengal Legislative Assembly voted in favour of Bengal's Partition in 1947:

> In the first joint voting, partition was rejected. But, by the second, the members from the Hindu majority areas accepted it. The number of legislators who decided the matter was farcical. Only seventy-nine members voted, and of them, fifty-eight voted for and twenty-one voted against partition. Thus the majority which brought it about was thirty-seven. All the Muslim members voted solidly against. I might repeat my lament that never was so much evil owing to so few...But as soon as the Bengalis realised the mistakes they had made, they completely repudiated their responsibility and began to blame the British, the Congress, Gandhi and Nehru for their misfortunes.

The story goes that Bengali Hindus, backed by both Congress and the Hindu Mahasabha, led by eminent leaders like Dr Shyama Prasad Mukherjee and Dr Prafulla Chandra Roy, were in favour of dividing Bengal, prompted by the atmosphere of fear instigated by the Noakhali riots. The movement against the prospect of Bengal going over to Pakistan gained credence owing to the Muslim League's dubious role in the riots. The Hindu legislators felt it necessary to oppose the League's campaign to secure the entire Bengal province. Communalization led to the formation of fear-centric camps in the beleaguered community, and gave free reign to the politics of fear and hatred.

On 1 January 1940, Gandhi wrote in *Harijan*: 'My belief is unshaken that without communal unity, Swaraj cannot be attained without non-violence. But unity cannot be reached without justice between communities. Muslim or any other friendship cannot be bought with bribery. Bribery would itself mean cowardice, and therefore violence…I can disarm suspicion only by being generous. Justice without generosity may easily be Shylock's justice.'

This is an extraordinary passage that throws light on Gandhi's ethical concerns, where he espouses an attitude of generosity which alone, he thought, would make the desire for justice meaningful. Justice here needs to be understood in political terms, as political justice. This makes the moving force behind generosity political, as much as ethical. We know Gandhi was willing to hear Jinnah's demands and find a way to convince both the Quaid-e-Azam and the Congress to reach an understanding about sharing power. His attempt should be read in the context of the above statement, where he rules out buying unity at all costs using cheap means.

Gandhi's failure to negotiate between Jinnah and the Congress may be read purely as a political failure. But it can also be seen, in the context of Gandhi's own intentions, as a failure of ethics in politics. It can be read as the limitation of ethical sensibilities like generosity in playing a decisive part in the politics of negotiation. Gandhi considers the question of justice through generosity not in any paternalistic sense, but as a condition of unity. He was earnestly placing the question of generosity against an atmosphere tainted with suspicion.

We need to pause here on the question of 'friendship'. In Gandhi's understanding, a host of qualities considered unethical or immoral—such as bribery, cowardice and violence—need to be given up, if one has to make a gesture of friendship. But bribery and violence are part of the political—they don't belong to an idea of ethics that exceeds politics. So is Gandhi looking for friendship in politics, between Hindus and Muslims, by demanding gestures that lie beyond—or in excess of—politics? Generosity is an ethical demand at the heart of politics. So is justice. Gandhi holds justice contingent upon generosity. But justice is related to law—something very precise, even though its reception may be imprecise and immense. However, generosity is immeasurable, and because of this, its relation to law is unaccountable.

What kind of justice does generosity bring? Is it infinite justice? A form of justice where the risks involved in seeking justice are incalculable (not measurable), and hence, in an ethical sense, infinite? Justice beyond (the) calculations (of history)? Justice that is unaccountable by law? Is such a justice possible in politics, within the Bismarckian idea of politics as 'the art of the possible'? If justice from generosity is incalculable, is it also impossible in politics? It is not the limits of generosity in politics that we need to awaken to, but the limits of politics in opening itself up, risking itself, for the sake of generosity. There is of course a politics *within* generosity, what we may call the politics of generosity, where we are pursued by calculations, and those calculations are political, limited by political considerations. But generosity allows negotiation, openness, and a possibility to break away from the strictly ideological stranglehold of politics. This is the difference between the Gandhian and other dominant forms of modern politics.

In *The Politics of Friendship*, Derrida asks: 'The friendship of a justice that transcends right [*le droit*], the law [*la loi*] of friendship above laws—is this acceptable? Acceptable in the name of precisely *what*? In the name of politics? Ethics? Law? Or in the name of a friendship which would no longer answer to any other agency than itself?' From Gandhi's demands and Derrida's questions, we may conclude that the question of justice between Hindus and Muslims can perhaps only be posed in its own name, where generosity overwhelms both history (not the lived history of the people, but the history of power) and law (the law of history and the law of the state, where we merely grapple with the problem of representation). Perhaps modern politics needs to include the shared vocabulary between neighbouring cultural traditions. This will help find more intimate and ethical ways to overcome the rationalist, political language of the West.

~

Man does not meet. He is the meeting.
—Emmanuel Levinas

The Urdu poet Ali Sardar Jafri narrated a story upon receiving the Jnanpith Award in 1997. It was a Bengali short story he had read years ago, but he had no recollection either of the author or the title. The story was set in rural Bengal. A group of women were bathing at the village pond, which was overlooked by a Durga temple on top of a hillock. Suddenly, the women heard a bangle-seller who was passing by call out to them. They eagerly invited him towards the bank. He settled down to sell his bangles, happy at his stroke of luck to find so many buyers in one place. The women came out of the pond one by one and bought bangles for themselves. As they left wearing his bangles, the satiated bangle-seller got ready to leave. Just then he heard a voice from the pond, 'Wait, what about me?' The bangle-seller turned to find the most beautiful woman he had ever seen, still left in the pond. How could he have missed her? Looking embarrassed, he asked the woman to come and take her pick. To the bangle-seller's surprise, the woman asked him to choose the bangles for her and also to help her wear them. The bangle-seller was only too glad to comply with her request. 'I think red bangles will best fit those fair arms,' he said, and put them on her. When he asked for the money, the woman said, 'I am afraid I don't have any money on me. But my father is a priest in the temple you see up there. If you tell him, he will give you the money.'

The bangle-seller walked up to the temple and met the priest. He told him about his daughter buying bangles from him and asked for the money. The priest was dumbfounded, 'What are you saying? My daughter? Where did you meet her?' The bangle-seller narrated the whole story. The priest ran towards the pond with the bangle-seller in tow. They found no one there. In a flash, the priest understood who the woman was and what had happened. He broke down crying, 'What sort of justice is this, mother? I spent my entire life in your worship, and you chose to give darshan to this bangle-seller?' The priest was inconsolable. Just then, the woman's hands appeared in the water, showing off her red bangles.

The Bengali story ended here, said Jafri. But he made a slight addition to the tale: that evening, when people gathered in the village mosque for namaz, the bangle-seller was also a part of the crowd. In Hindustan, as we know, bangles are traditionally sold by Muslims. Jafri's addition does not merely add a sociological detail to the story. It grants the story a richly-layered meaning that brings various affinities together.

In Jafri's retelling of the Bengali story, the idea of darshan, in a radical turn, moves beyond the social and cultural codes within a religious community and embraces the field of an encounter between the Hindu and the Muslim. This encounter is also ethically demanding, as it looks to discover ways of acceptability between two different orders of faith.

Without Jafri's addition to the tale, one may situate the reasons behind the goddess giving darshan to a bangle-seller in moral terms, as a mark of favouring humility against vanity. In concrete terms, humility here also gets associated with people belonging to an underprivileged caste and class. Vanity is seen as a mark of the Brahminical elite. It makes a corresponding—and critical—social and cultural distinction, reversing the relation between (cultural) power and (moral) value, thus opening up the possibilities of a political reading of the story. But the story still remains within the context of the Hindu community. Jafri's addition widens the context of the story by extending the discourse of value and power to the domain of the Hindu-Muslim encounter.

The idea of darshan is strictly Hindu, as the idea of divinity in Islam exists without a form. What is crucial in Jafri's retelling is not the Muslim bangle-seller not seeing his encounter with the goddess as darshan, but the priest's belief that the goddess he worshipped all his life chose to appear before someone outside his social class, caste, and even religion. It is the priest's moment of truth, where he finds himself humbled, though whether it instilled any degree of humility in him or not is conjectural. The feeling of being betrayed by the goddess may not necessarily translate to a recognition of his prejudices.

Jafri's retelling conveys a lesson by using a subject who is outside its religious context, but who is nevertheless related in cultural, historical and ethical terms. The Muslim bangle-seller, being outside the shared symbolic world of the goddess and the Brahmin priest, helps illuminate the priest's moral and ethical shortcomings. The point is, for the priest the incident was an act of darshan, while the bangle-seller experienced it, at best, as a spell of beauty. And yet, by tricking (and escaping) both the bangle-seller and the priest, the goddess manages to impart an ethical lesson, without herself turning into a fetishized object of worship.

There is playfulness written into the script of darshan in both instances in the story: the goddess wearing the bangles from the Muslim bangle-seller and then showing them off to the priest. Her resistance against becoming a fetishized object of worship is doubly reinforced when she reappears, assuaging the priest's complaint a little bit by showing him her bangled hands. Here there is playfulness along with the political message that she has accepted the bangles from an ordinary man (of another caste/class/religion). The image is paradoxical from the priest's point of view: a trace of darshan that comes as a token of benevolence, with the disturbing lesson that it does not belong to him alone. The ethical lesson in this legendary encounter between goddess and bangle-seller works at various levels: a) the primacy of simplicity over the sacred privileges of priesthood, b) the event of darshan being outside the calculability and ego of the worshipper, and c) legendary, spiritual encounters also being part of history, where an ethical gesture involves welcoming the other.

The Spanish poet Antonio Machado, quoted by Octavio Paz, left behind an evocative passage on the meaning of the other in history: 'The other does not exist: this is rational faith, the incurable belief of human reason. Identity=Reality, as if, in the end, everything must necessarily and absolutely be one and the same. But the other refuses to disappear; it subsists, it persists, it is the hard bone on which reason breaks its teeth. Abel Martín, with a poetic faith, as human as rational faith, believed in the other, in "The essential Heterogeneity of being," in what might be called the incurable otherness from which oneness must always suffer.' Identity is trapped in self-referential manoeuvre. Whereas the other poses itself as a relation, (over)shadowing the limits of identity, a poetic counterpart to reason, the *you* that counters the *I* of language, tempting and disturbing (the laws of) identity.

The idea of darshan in the Bengali story retold by Jafri moves away from the world of 'rational faith' into the realm of 'poetic faith', where one faces—grudgingly or soberly—the presence of the other. What is poetic faith in this or any other context? It is perhaps closer to the meaning of messianic faith that Derrida defined in *Spectres of Marx* as 'the experience of the impossible, which can only be a radical experience of the perhaps.'

Both the priest and the bangle-seller experienced a moment *outside* the everyday, whose meaning is both speculative and mysterious, albeit haunted by the presence of beauty. Their respective rational faiths are incapable of drawing meanings about the incident that brought both of them together. The woman who fled the scene left them with a number of questions they need to find answers for. The story forces us to ponder on the relationship between the Hindu and the Muslim. This relationship is best understood in the terms of radical alterity or otherness, not in its abstract philosophical sense but in its concrete, cultural, everyday sense—of living side by side, of the other as part of one's (cultural) neighbourhood. There is a palpable nearness between these two names that are *other* to each other, Hindu and Muslim; they are *perhaps* closer than we think.

If darshan, as a Hindu mode of performative faith, and messianism, as a term having affinity with the Abrahamic religions, can both be manifestations of 'poetic faith', certainly a dialogue can emerge from within these discourses. For poetic faith alone, Machado's apocryphal character Abel Martin says, recognizes the presence of the other. It is this poetic faith that has its residue in the future, for it leaves behind questions that the limitations and prejudices of 'rational faith' have to address. The idea of rational faith, after all, equates self with reality, trapped within the structure and ethos of the singular subject.

The presence of the other, which expands (by challenging) one's notion of faith (in oneself), allows the question of the 'perhaps' to come into the world, into one's thought. It is the element of 'perhaps' brought about by Jafri's sociological addition that enriches the Bengali story. This 'perhaps' draws the characters of the bangle-seller and priest together, even though their relationship with the goddess is different.

There is another anecdote that may further illustrate the relationship between ethics, poetic faith and the Hindu-Muslim relationship in India.

It is a story of my meeting with the famous Sufi qawwal from Karachi, Farid Ayaz. I caught him in his tent at the India International Centre, where he had come to take part in a festival on Kabir. After initial greetings, I requested him for a photograph. He displayed mock hesitation by singing aloud, 'Meri tasveer lekar kya karoge?' (What will you do by taking my photograph?). It sounded like the first line of a possible ghazal. I found myself inspired to reply in his style, 'Ek Kafirana shauk pura karenge' (I will fulfil the pleasure of a Kafir). Ayaz's eyes lit up, he smiled, and said with lyrical emphasis, 'Par hum to Kafir ko w-a-h-a-n dhoond rahe thhe...' (But I was looking *there* for the Kafir), pointing towards the horizon with his finger. It was my turn to smile, as I completed the exchange, 'Aur dekhiye, hum yahin mil gaye...' (And see, you find me right here).

Perhaps this encounter yields many obvious secrets behind the ethical possibilities between the Hindu and the Muslim. When Ayaz pointed to the horizon, stressing on the word 'w-a-h-a-n' (there), I was reminded of the 'horizon' in Levinas's discourse on ethics. It is on the 'horizon' that one meets the other. This meeting entails a waiting as much as a hearing, endlessly postponing the bloodshed of history and the self-centric certainties of 'rational faith'. If history cannot solve our problems we have to stop listening to it for answers. For the only answer it has always offered us is violence, a violence that refuses to meet, or hear, the other.

Perhaps, with poetic faith at our disposal, we have to trust the meeting where, as Levinas suggested, we are ourselves the meeting, ourselves consisting what we mean by meeting, we are always on our way to that place where we become something (else) through meeting. The Hindu-Muslim relationship needs to exhaust its ethical possibilities, not by disregarding or forgetting history, but, hearing what it constantly fails to tell us about each other. The historical task of the Hindu is to look for the Muslim and for the Muslim it is to look for the Hindu. The task is historical but the demand is ethical: to find a way out of history. This way out of history is obviously *within* history, but it opens up another horizon where identitarian forms of nationalism and other ideological hazards don't intervene in an older, much less constructed language of communicability, and where reason plays second fiddle to affectivity. Just as in the Bengali story narrated by Jafri, despite his inconsolable disappointment, the Brahmin priest's jealousy towards the Muslim bangle-seller does not end in violent acrimony. The priest's sentiments work within the familiar economy of a shared, cultural milieu, where he experiences being humbled by his divinity, who favoured someone from a different religion. The grand history of conflicts tramples such narratives where we discover the more intimate clues to people's lives. To find a way out of history, we have to go back to those narratives.

~

O my sad heart, hear what I have to say
Where I find no respite, there I won't stay
—Sahir Ludhianvi, *Funtoosh* (1956)

Saadat Hasan Manto, who has written the starkest stories of Partition, after moving to Lahore in January, 1948 from his beloved city Bombay, could not find his way out of history. Manto was a scriptwriter in Bombay's film industry in the 1940s. When his friend, the legendary actor Ashok Kumar, and his producer-partner, Suvik Wacha, took over Bombay Talkies, they offered—in a redeeming gesture that resisted the septic atmosphere of communal violence and disharmony—the most senior positions to Muslims. For this, Wacha received mails threatening arson and murder. But he and Kumar stuck to their guns. Despite such a show of solidarity by friends, the atmosphere was perhaps poisoned beyond redemption for Manto when he discovered his Hindu friend Shyam had violent feelings against him after they heard together stories of communal violence from a Sikh family who had escaped from Rawalpindi. It was a major personal incident that fuelled Manto's decision to leave the Bombay he loved, for Pakistan.

Another famous, left-wing writer of those times, Josh Malihabadi, much admired by Nehru, finally shifted to Pakistan in 1958 despite his intense reluctance to leave India. Malihabadi, besides his growing concern about the fate of Muslims, was also deeply disturbed about the future of Urdu in India. Nehru made keen efforts to make him stay, even suggesting he travel back and forth whenever he liked, but Malihabadi was torn by the practicalities. He finally succumbed to the wisdom of his friend and chief commissioner of Karachi, Syed Abu Talib Naqvi, who told him, 'Josh saheb, you can't cross a river with your feet anchored in two boats.'

In Malihabadi's own narration, his meetings with Maulana Abdul Kalam Azad made him apprehensive about staying in India once Nehru was no more. He shared those fears with the prime minister, but the 'narrow-minded patriotism of the Hindus', which Nehru thought his poet-friend could ignore, proved decisive for Malihabadi. In a tearing nazm on his departure, Malihabadi writes about the landscape of Malihabad, detailing each tree like a gardener, embracing his loss, registering the death of ties between landscape and man, a 'live corpse, carried off from home'. The poet leaves the echo of his name behind.

From Manto's and Malihabadi's examples, it is clear that the desire to leave one's own country does not only come from a real or perceived threat to life. It also comes from a radical breakdown of trust. When Manto, as he recounted in his memoir, asked his friend Shyam if after hearing the stories of Muslim atrocities he wanted to kill him, Shyam replied, 'Not now, but when I was listening to them...I could have killed you.'

Manto understood the 'psychological background' of the 'communal holocaust of Partition' from Shyam's desire to kill him when he was hearing the story, but not later. It told him that communal feelings can cast a spell where both objectivity and friendliness are eclipsed by an overwhelming sense of hate. In that mindless moment, a person's religious identity is implicated without moral, ethical and even affective registers of belonging. The person is stripped of all human meanings that made the friendship possible in the first place. The fact that the person who goes through that moment of intense hate calms down later, only proves the fatal, if momentary, nature of the illness. The shock of that revelation led to Manto's departure.

The growing communalization of Hindu-Muslim relations today is reminiscent of what happened during Manto and Malihabadi's time. Trust is thrown into the cesspool of jingoism.

In *The Other Side of Silence: Voices from the Partition of India*, Urvashi Butalia writes about women being abducted, raped, converted, and forced into marriages and prostitution during episodes of mass violence. Butalia writes, 'The Organiser wasn't quite prepared to admit that Hindu and Sikh men had been guilty of abductions.' Even debates in the constituent assembly treated it as an 'aberration'. Muslim men alone were demonized for sexual crimes against women during Partition. Both the (secular) Indian state and the Hindu Right treated the matter with moral hypocrisy. This hypocrisy was necessary to render the foundations of the nation honourable. What this hypocrisy managed to forcibly remove is the possibility of regathering trust. Instead of Hindus and Muslims sharing collective grief as a mode of healing the wounds of Partition, a collective pride is kept in place to ensure that the narrative of Partition is alive. A nation is also what a nation forgets, as it pretends to remember its past. It becomes a more 'honourable' option to memorialize the myth and debunk the shame of independence.

Trust was a forgotten value after 30 January 1948. The secular politics of the Nehruvian state was sincere about minority rights and mutual toleration. But the importance of trust was lost with Gandhi's death. There was nobody to say, like Gandhi did in *Young India* on 4 June 1925, 'I believe in trusting. Trust begets trust. Suspicion is fetid and only stinks. He who trusts has never yet lost in the world.' Hindus and

Muslims, during Partition and after, have been prepared to lose, for the sake of pride, what they could have gained by trusting each other. The secular state is only suited to solve matters of dispute between two communities. It cannot provide ways to engage with (or overcome) deeper matters of trust and reconciliation. For the secular state itself is implicated in the moral mess that founded the nation. In the name of instating a social order, the secular state overlooked its responsibilities regarding the ethical issue of trust.

The foundation of social order is most often a fiction guarded by law. The necessity for such an order needs to be supplemented by public expiation. No law can ensure peace without setting an example of social honesty. In time, the unfulfilled possibility of that honesty degenerates into acceptance of mass crimes. This is testified by Hindu men bragging on tape about rapes they committed during the 2002 Gujarat pogroms.

In contrast to this degenerate state of Hindu-Muslim relations, imagine Manto's exceptional friendship with Ashok Kumar. In his memoir, Manto recounts the day when 'religious killings were...at their height' (he does not offer a date, but it must have been post-August 1947). He was returning with Ashok Kumar from Bombay Talkies, and had spent a few hours at Kumar's residence. Kumar offered to drop Manto home, and they ended up passing through a Muslim neighbourhood, where a marriage procession was passing by. Manto was scared to bits, 'praying in broken words', invoking god to dissuade any act of violence that would render him guilty for life. Manto feared that if Kumar was harmed, the country would never forgive him. A few people in the crowd recognized Kumar and shouted his name. Manto froze. He was prepared to reveal his identity in order to avoid disaster. Then two men rushed towards the car and, ignoring Manto, addressed Kumar, 'Ashok bhai, this street will lead you nowhere. It is best to turn into this side lane.'

The fragile and exemplary nature of this story reveals a couple of key aspects in our political history. At a personal level, friendship inspired Ashok Kumar to risk driving through a Muslim neighbourhood at the height of Hindu-Muslim riots to drop Manto home. Friendship inspires trust, and trust emboldens the spirit. Despite the breakdown of social relations, a Muslim crowd in Bombay displayed an affectionate attitude towards Ashok Kumar. It was perhaps not merely the respect Kumar had earned as a popular figure of Indian cinema, but also what the culture of the Bombay film industry represented in the minds of people. It was a culture where Urdu and Hindi thrived together as languages, as much as Hindu and Muslim filmmakers, actors, music directors, lyricists and singers. To take just one example: Sahir Ludhianvi's most memorable compositions were set to tune by Sachin Dev Burman in Guru Dutt's *Pyasa*, and the songs were sung by Mohammad Rafi and Geeta Dutt. The history of the Bombay film industry is a reflection of our folk and popular cultural history, where spiritual beliefs, social criticism of those beliefs, legendary love stories and the idea of love and friendship, overlap religions and cultures. Any attempt to engineer a culturally fascist agenda of segregating languages, stories and sensibilities cannot last.

Recently, abysmally crude attempts were made by singers and others in the Hindi film industry, to play flagbearers for the Hindu Right, and compensate for their flagging careers. They did not achieve much besides making fools of themselves and earning the disgust of liberal-secular fans. But for an uncomfortably brief while, such voices of hate, along with social media trolls, were publicly accusing Indian Muslims (including Muslim film stars) of having their hearts in Pakistan. In the Bombay film industry, people largely stay away from politics. Politics is seen as antithetical to business, as the industry survives purely on economic fortunes. Over the years, famous actors and actresses have, however, often dabbled in politics. In recent times, the politician-film star nexus has been in the news more often, each party using the other for promotional activities. Such games of convenience raise eyebrows and spark controversies. Even though film stars may stay away from politics, they do hold political views like the rest of the society, and often air them publicly on social media and other platforms. Shahrukh Khan was hounded for supporting protests by writers and artists on national television. Aamir Khan faced the wrath of Hindu nationalists, after he aired his wife Kiran Rao's apprehensions about staying on in the country, scared for their children's safety in the prevailing atmosphere of intimidation and violence. It does not occur to those who are sick with their discomfort with Pakistan, that they alone are pathologically obsessed with that country.

For nationalists, the remembering of Partition is not an occasion for regret, empathy or mourning. It is an occasion to rake up selectively chosen wounds and relive those moments of collective horror. On the one hand, Hindu nationalism extols the rhetoric of sentiments, and on the other, refuses to find a way to heal these wounds. Liberal and left-wing nationalists are caught in the secular/religious distinction that prevents them from addressing the dormant wounds of the community. The idea of memory and its persistence in the life of a community eludes the rationalist sensibility of liberal and Left ideologues. No wonder the right wing has managed to exploit it for its own divisive agenda. There is a popular as well as intellectual need to honestly confront the history of violence, outside the duplicities of nationalist logic, so that a new idea of history can emerge from the stories of lived experiences. This other history of the everyday, where neighbourly trust existed, can be reaffirmed, its denial acknowledged, only by rearticulating the collective trauma of Partition.

The inability to mourn a horror is the surest way to repeat it.

4

The Nation's Untouchables

The 'notion' of untouchability is most visible, most embodied, in touch. Analyzing the phenomenology of touch in the encounter between the touchable and the untouchable, we realize the role of stigma in violating affective norms between the outcast and the upper-caste Hindu. The non-relationship trembles at the margins of a peculiar law that prevents both sense and sensibility from overcoming artificial codes of exclusion. If touch suffers under the scanner of stigma, labour suffers devaluation. We receive the terrible impression of how the touchable body lives an absurd life to maintain the code of untouchability. We study the Gandhian movement in relation to this problem, where older norms of untouchability were readjusted within a new politics (and ethics) of touchability. We then meditate on the suicide of the iconic Dalit scholar, Rohith Vemula, who paid the price for defying the politics of caste and Hindu nationalism. In the last section, we return to Ambedkar's proposal for the annihilation of caste and untouchability, where we consider his arguments in favour of conversion.

It was the high priest of Hindu revivalism in the late nineteenth century, Vivekananda, who in a rare outburst of critical honesty wrote:

> We are neither Vedantists, most of us now, nor Pauranics nor Tantrics. We are just "Don't-touchists"…Our God is in

the cooking-pot, and our religion is, "Don't touch me, I am holy." If this goes on for another century, every one of us will be in a lunatic asylum.

The most notable aspect of the caste system is that the norms laid down to define what constitutes it are derived from its exception, from what lies outside it. This is what Ambedkar tried to explain in a note to Gandhi, published in *Harijan* on 7 February 1933: 'The Out-caste is a by-product of the Caste system. There will be outcastes as long as there are castes. Nothing can emancipate the Out-caste except the destruction of the Caste system.' In the same vein, the norms of touch and touchability come from the limits of touch, from the exception that is deemed untouchable. To echo Ambedkar's flawless inverse logic that only the abolition of the system of castes would correspondingly ensure the abolition of the figure of the outcaste, the problem of untouchability can be erased by erasing the sanctified conventions of touch in Hindu society.

Throughout history, people have been declared untouchables owing to their proximity to dead bodies and filth of various kinds, including human faeces. These were mostly occupational hazards, which were fixed as markers of these people's identities. They were consequently turned into social outcasts. Hindus have the most prejudiced—apart from the more universally hierarchical—notion of occupation in history. In the 2016 anti-reservation stir against the government's proposed 27 per cent reservation for Other Backward Castes in medical and engineering colleges, upper-caste medical college students in Delhi showed the attitude merit-loving Hindus have towards menial labour. Trainee doctors protested with brooms, to showcase their crass sarcasm. For those who use the stethoscope, the broom is a lowly tool of labour.

Labour is what labour touches. Hindu society hierarchizes labour by valuing some and devaluing other forms of labour.

Ambedkar points out that the caste system, involves not only a division of labour, but also a 'division of labourers'. It is also the stigmatized division of the tools of labour. Anything that smelled bad to the Hindu became a source of paranoid repulsion. The caste system is, in many ways, a system organized around smells, where the sensation of smelling gets entwined with the idea of touching.

People who deal with substances giving off bad smells mark their own untouchability. The Hindu's other is an olfactory other, where notions of smell colour the idea of touch. Aristotle, in his elaboration of aesthesis in *De Anima* (On the Soul), considered touch as primordial, animalistic, and therefore the basest among human faculties. The Hindus turned touch, in contrast, into something sacred, but only in terms of prohibition: most things were not about touch but about 'not touching'. To touch or not to touch has been the central spiritual predicament in the lives of Hindus.

Aristotle relegates touch to the lower order of human perception, but he does mention it as a mark of the superior intelligence of human beings in comparison to animals, and a faculty that enhances aesthetic potential. A keen sense of smell, in the Aristotelian understanding, adds to this discriminatory/aesthetic power of touch in human beings. There is a tacit assumption in Aristotle that aligns the sensuous notion of touch and smell with the familiar, and the discriminatory notion with the unfamiliar. Yet human beings have shown a far greater capacity for adapting to and welcoming unfamiliar smells, and making unfamiliar objects touchable, than Aristotle could imagine.

The untouchables, as Ambedkar explained, are not merely the impure who are kept away during ceremonial occasions. Untouchables pollute everything at all times. It is one of the defining moments of Hindu law. Sundar Sarukkai, in his perceptive essay, 'Phenomenology of Untouchability', makes two important observations in this regard. Citing Derrida's *On Touching: Jean-Luc Nancy*, Sarukkai discusses his equation between untouchability and law. Derrida brings in the notion of 'tact' as the first notion of the law. Tact, for Derrida, creates a paradox around touch, being a notion of 'touch without touching'. So tact introduces a respect for the law that, in turn, forces two people to be tactful about touching each other. Sarukkai finds that the problem of untouchability in India lies beyond this situation of tactful touchability. The untouchable is not the autonomous subject of touch that is present in the West, in relation to 'objects of touch' like law, or emerging from a certain sense of 'incompleteness', existential or sensuous. She has no autonomy to choose in this regard, whether she can touch what is untouchable *for her*, or not. She encounters a codified realm, sanctioned by Hindu social law, where she is relegated outside the territory of touching. Also, Sarukkai observes, 'the impulse against touching is situated within the "object", the untouchable'.

So if the body of the Brahmin is the body and the source of law, the body of the untouchable is the subject of law. But paradoxically, it is the Brahmin's body which is rendered untouchable by law, because it is the Brahmin who has codified his own body within his own law. The untouchable's body alone holds the promise of touch, the promise of a subject whose sensuous impulses are denied by the Brahminical body of law. In other words, it is by annihilating its promise of touch that the untouchable subject is forced to fulfil its pact with the law of untouchability. In the case of untouchability, the law draws its spirit from the history of segregation in Hindu society, where rules of exclusion are premised upon 'notions' of touch and smell. In other words, they are established by rules based on prejudice. This pre-judicial judgement in the case of untouchability puts this abominable system of beliefs and practices into the sphere of prejudice. It reconfirms Ambedkar's bewilderment regarding the unique feature of what he called 'hereditary Untouchability': something that is born of prejudice, to sanction a pre-legal law.

However, the problem of touch remains. The denial of touch is as haunting as the desire for touch. In the context of purity, of maintaining pure bodies, the element of touch works in insidious ways. What is a pure body? Extending an insight by Merleau-Ponty, that to touch is always *also* touching one's own self, a reversible experience, Sarukkai explains that the Brahmin body, by practising untouchability, makes itself untouchable. The 'pure' Brahmin body is a 'folded body', an expression which Sarukkai invokes from Gopal Guru. This predicament, of losing touch with oneself, is what Sarukkai calls 'the potential untouchability…of one-self'. If the sphere of touchability is also the sphere where the fear of untouchability lurks, it is a sphere of annulled potentiality. The Hindu is a paradoxical animal who turns himself potentially untouchable.

In his essay, 'The Ellipsis of Touch: Gandhi's Unequals,' Aishwary Kumar quotes Gandhi, who tries to distinguish between the general principles of impurity and hereditary untouchability: 'Every time my mother handled unclean things she became untouchable for the time being and had to cleanse herself by bathing…I refuse to believe that anyone can be regarded untouchable by reason of his or her birth, and such untouchability as recognized by religion is by its very nature transitory—easily removable and referable to the deed and not the doer.' By leaving a justifiable space for what Kumar calls 'transitory and necessary untouchability' in relation to ceremonial and other everyday practices, Gandhi leaves intact the Hindu culture of paranoid excesses regarding touch.

Kumar quotes Gandhi again, throwing up a further

complication in his stand against hereditary untouchability: 'Does untouchability in the case of a cobbler or scavenger attach to birth or occupation? If it attaches to birth, it is hideous and must be rooted out; but if it attaches to occupation it may be a sanitary rule of great importance. It is of universal application...the scavenger's children may remain scavengers without being or feeling degraded and they will be no more considered untouchables than Brahmins. The fault does not therefore lie in recognizing the law of hereditary transmission of qualities from generation to generation, but it lies with the faulty conception of inequality.'

It is interesting to note two immediate things: one, Gandhi regards sanitary rules as a permanent feature across time; two, without making an issue out of the law of heredity, Gandhi deflects the matter onto a universal question: the moral principle of equality. Kumar reads Gandhi's conception of inequality as one where there is a lack of acknowledgment of each other's skills, his idea of equality being the production and dissemination of knowledge across vocations. But, as Kumar goes on to argue, the Gandhian satyagrahi practised a 'sacrosanct and ironic untouchability' by calling the untouchable 'Harijan', children of god.

In his essay, 'Gandhi and His Fast', Ambedkar rejects the name 'Harijan': 'The Untouchables simply detest the name Harijan...The new name provides no escape to the Untouchables from the curse of untouchability. With the new name they are damned as much as they were with the old. Secondly, the Untouchables say that they prefer to be called Untouchables. They argue that it is better that the wrong should be called by its known name...The new name in so far as it is concealment is fraud upon the Untouchables and a false absolution to the Hindus. Thirdly, there is also the feeling that the name Harijan is indicative of pity.' The new name bestowed by Gandhi, Ambedkar argues, is not really new, as it does nothing more than *conceal* the condition of the untouchables. It is not the name but what is 'wrong' in its name that needs to be eliminated first. Renaming the untouchable thus merely ensured a wrong impression for both upper-caste Hindus and untouchables, and a prolonging of caste as a 'wrong relationship', to use a phrase from *Annihilation*.

Gandhi did not *begin* by referring to untouchables as 'Harijan'. He used the word 'Antyaja' on 16 January 1925, first in a speech at a women's conference at Sojitra, a village in Gujarat, and for many years, after till as late as 23 November 1932, in a letter to Narandas Gandhi. In his speech at the women's conference, Gandhi reiterated how his mother and wife would become Antyaja 'for some time', which as noted earlier by Kumar, was Gandhi's accepted form of 'transitory and necessary untouchability'. In the letter to Narandas, Gandhi spoke about the Dalit weaver, Ramji G. Badhia, 'We should not feel hurt by anything he says. We should even put up with insults from him. All this is part of our atonement (for our treatment of the Antyajas).' On 11 February 1933, Gandhi explained in *Harijan*, the meaning of—and his preference for— the word 'Harijan', where god is invoked as the 'Friend of the friendless' and the 'Protector of the weak'. Gandhi's change in addressing the untouchable, from 'Antyaja' to 'Harijan', marks a shift from the historical to the exemplary. The Antyaja was now transformed into a special subject. This special subject however was no longer the subject of a whole history of hurt and humiliation. The word 'Harijan' took away the historical ground of the untouchable subject, and granted him a new status *within* the Hindu fold. Gandhi's idea of establishing equality was to find a point (or a name) that stood outside the sphere of history, discarding the nomenclature of inequality and exclusion. With the name 'Harijan', Gandhi invented a paradox in relation to the problem: he freed the untouchable from the stigma attached to her name, but only by, once again, *naming* her. As if the untouchable cannot (re)name her own self, and use the agency of her own imagination to get out of this historical predicament.

In Kumar's analysis, Gandhi's Harijan, in her capacity of being 'superiorly' unequal, merely became 'the sacred message of one satyagrahi to another', without being able to intervene in that creative circuit of satyagraha. In other words, the Harijan entered as a divine surplus into the social and ethical economy of satyagraha. She was a new, alien figure, dislocating her history of exclusion from *Antyaja* to untouchable, by introducing the possibility of an incomplete transcendence.

The deepest problem of this Gandhian truce is, Kumar points out: 'For Gandhi, the only possible measure of equality among unequals, a measure that did not violate the unequal's difference and disrespect his forced poverty, was hinged on the satyagrahi's embrace of equality through his own voluntary sacrifice, or *tyag*.' Upper-caste Hindus were to gain moral agency through their efforts to equalize relations. What of the Harijan? Gandhi's satyagraha sought to bypass the historical possibility of restoring equality between upper-caste Hindus and untouchables, by bringing in a sensuous possibility of emancipation, by creating new conditions of touchability. The name 'Harijan' was a way out of the historical trap, by elevating the untouchable's signifier without considering the material history of oppression *as such*. At the same time, it rendered the memory of that history unaccounted for and unnecessary. This forgetting lies at the heart of the satyagrahic paradox, where the demands of touchability weighed upon the *reminder* of inequality, through the trapped figure of the unequal.

Even though Gandhi brings the untouchable and the

satyagrahi within the sphere of touchability, the untouchable ends up being 'the exemplary hostage and unequal witness to satyagraha'. For Gandhi, the primary necessity is of a shared moral order between castes, expressed through registers of empathy and sacrifice. The 'elliptical and ethical violence of ahimsa', for Kumar, lies in the privileged castes and the untouchable being made to forcibly reside within an idea of life (and inequality) which averts violence against the (untouchable, unequal) other in the name of sacrifice. The idea of sacrifice dictates the limit-situation of satyagraha.

There is one conceptual puzzle left to ponder regarding the problem of touch and untouchability among the Hindus. In their world of 'active' untouchability, how does the body survive the restrictions imposed on itself: its daily rituals of don't-touch-this and don't-touch-that, of don't-touch-him-or-her, of don't-touch-now-or-never? How does a Hindu, in his asylum of don't-touchism, survive the lunacy of his self-proclaimed holiness? The answer lies in the Hindus' denial of the body, and their bizarre division of bodies into pure and impure, which derives its norm by declaring its exception—the shadow—as untouchable too. It is not merely the body of the untouchable that cannot be touched—it is also the untouchable's shadow. This world of bodies is one where the disembodied shadow of the untouchable has a body, and her body is a disembodied shadow of itself. This is the Brahminical shadow-game.

A shadow is where light does not fall. But since the shadow has the shape of the body, the attributes of the body are extended to the shadow. This is a hallucinatory perception of a double-bind where bodies are shadows and shadows bodies. Hindus live in the shadow of a touch, feeling touched by shadows. Everyone lives inside Plato's allegorical cave of flitting shadows. Such a primitive condition prevents the quasi-

Aristotelian subject, discriminating through touch, from getting out of the Platonic parable of ignorance. Even though Hindus pray to the sun every morning, the sunlight has not released the dark hubris hiding in their bodies. The Hindu body is a slave to the hallucinatory moksha of its soul.

In our times, these violent contradictions were exposed in the most historic manner—apart from the many Dalit writings and protests—by the suicide note of a Dalit student. The abrupt yet coherent language of the note, its dignified sarcasm, its indictment of those who lacked the cultural resources to recognize the world as a place where particles of the universe are born to dream, and its decisive bid to escape the stranglehold of a disappointing reality, shook readers across the world.

~

So the future lies in darkness and the forces of right
Are weak. All this was plain to you
When you destroyed a torturable body.

—Bertolt Brecht,
'On the Suicide of the Refugee W.B.'

These lines by Brecht, from his poem on the German-Jewish philosopher and literary critic, Walter Benjamin, tell us a person committing suicide has one terrible advantage at his disposal: his clarity. In Benjamin's case, it was not simply clarity about his personal situation, being unable to pass through border checkposts and fearing he would be turned over to the Nazis. It was also the darkened vision of a future which Benjamin carried before his eyes, for a racist regime was ruling his country and hope had receded beyond the horizon. In Vladimir Mayakovsky's last poem, 'Past One O'Clock', written two nights before he shot himself, the clarity is equally chilling—he was caught between a Stalinist regime discrediting his poetry and a failed love affair. Paul Celan was driven to the same fate also, for more reasons than one: a mediocre poet's wife accusing him of plagiarism, and his psychiatric treatment. But the poet might also have been referring to the larger web of desolation of being Jewish in postwar Europe, when he wrote two months before he jumped into the Seine: 'They have healed me to pieces.'

A twenty-five-year-old Dalit scholar from the University of Hyderabad, Rohith Vemula, who committed suicide on 17 January 2016, also left a stunning note for his friends and the world alike, whose content is full of serious lessons for India's caste-ridden society. A sequence of unfortunate events led Rohith to end his life in his friend Uma Maheshwar's room. It all started after he participated in a small protest against the disruption of a film screening on the Muzaffarnagar riots in Delhi University by the Akhil Bharatiya Vidyarthi Parishad (ABVP), a Hindu right-wing student organization. Can't a film showing atrocities against religious minorities be screened in a country which boasts of being the world's largest democracy? Rohith was well within his rights to protest against majoritarian vandalism. When he was suspended by university authorities for an alleged assault on a fellow student, which was never proven beyond doubt, he must have felt the world closing in around him. The accusation of being 'casteist, extremist and anti-national' by a Union Minister in a letter must have broken his heart. How can a Dalit, who is a victim of casteism, be casteist? The game of casteism is prone to absurd charges, and Rohith's intelligence couldn't make sense of it.

In the note, he writes, 'I feel a growing gap between my soul and my body. And I have become a monster.' He goes on to say where his soul lay—in becoming a writer of science like Carl Sagan. But he got entangled in politics. Rohith realized that he had lost ties with his soul, when he was reminded of his body, named under the fixed categories of caste politics. He realized the contradiction between the flights of his writerly soul and his tortured material existence. His body had been dragged into the arena of caste politics. The new regime of religious nationalists was particularly brutal. The Hindu Right has the fiercest paranoia and revulsion against any form of anti-caste assertion. Rohith was caught in a historic moment when the insurgent spirit of Dalit politics locked horns with the growing fangs of Hindutva.

Fourteen days after his suspension notice was confirmed on 3 January 2016, in the middle of a relay hunger strike, Rohith took his life. Life had been a daily battleground where body and soul were growing apart. To ask a genuinely naive question, was he too philosophical for politics? I ask this question because he felt politics had no place for his soul. Rohith wanted to think in another direction, where he could imagine the universe, where thought was universal. Instead he was trapped by a different science: the science (and politics) of untouchability, bound to the law of heredity, where the soul is all body and the body a reflection of its shadow.

For Rohith, the politics of humiliation had come to overshadow the world of the soul. His soul was in the stars and in nature. These objects expanded the horizon of imagination, or what Guru calls the 'life of the mind', a phrase used by Hannah Arendt to describe how the mind works in relation to body and soul. In his obituary for Rohith, Guru emphasized his words about lives where the 'life of the mind motivates one to develop ambitions for ideas, this seeking to outgrow narrow caste identities and to become part of a universal idea.' This 'universal idea' need not necessarily be based on reason. It can arrive from the intuition of equality and freedom. Politics, on the contrary, reduced the value of a man 'to his immediate identity and nearest possibility.' Politics is neither universal, nor natural, in relation to the speculative sphere of science, where you make enquiries into nature and the cosmos. Rohith faced the politics of 'identity', which never allows one to be *other*.

Politics which tears the soul from the body, was not for him. He lamented that he loved nature and people, without knowing that people were long divorced from nature. This is quite a Rousseauian angst, pretty late into the very heart, or heartlessness, of the post-industrial era. What Rohith understood as valuable in a man meant nothing to the world around him, beyond the constraints of his identity and its restricted possibilities. Rohith was a Dalit, and it came in the way of his quest for the stars. Being Dalit was Rohith's only value for upper-caste Hindus, a value measured only through denial, insult and injury.

How to understand Rohith's use of the word 'soul', in relation to the material condition that put his life (the life of the body) under severe constraints? Even if we dismiss all the saints' and philosophers' theories of the soul as an entity, we are still left with the amorphous idea which Fernando Pessoa called 'a hidden orchestra', and in his novel *Blindness*, José Saramago described as: 'Inside us there is something that has no name, that something is what we are.' That something in Rohith, that something he recognized as his soul, was his value. The soul is full of possibilities, is *something*. It is the true measure of immeasurability, something akin to the wonder of realizing yourself to be a 'glorious thing made up of star dust', where you inhabit the spirit of (cosmic) transcendence. In that, Rohith betrays a clarity which Brecht saw in Benjamin, and which Mayakovsky and Celan saw in themselves.

It was this value which he found reduced: 'To a vote. To a number. To a thing.' A thing is the opposite of an evocative and unspecified 'something'. To exist as a thing is to be torn from possibilities. He felt neglected as a mind everywhere, 'in streets, in politics and in dying and living'. The instrumentality of life merged with the instrumentality of politics. Rohith was aghast at the total death of possibilities in the world. He was violated by the reduction to a number and a thing to be counted, a number wearing an identity mark forced around his neck.

Yet, Rohith reminds us, the moment of his birth is irreconcilable, a 'fatal accident'. Despite that catastrophe—being saddled with a caste that foreshadowed all his troubles—Rohith was chased by history's shadow, which envelopes many young lives struggling for their place under the sun.

One such life belonged to Muthukrishnan Jeevanathan, a Dalit research scholar studying history at Jawaharlal Nehru University, who committed suicide in March 2017. Though he did not leave a suicide note, his writings on social media clearly indicated how he experienced this structural bias. On his 6 July 2016 Facebook post, Muthukrishnan wrote how he hadn't picked up 'English properly. But I tried because I just don't want to give up.' Sitting below the statue of Nehru in the JNU campus, he faced his own question, 'Why you don't want to educate me?' The English language was Muthukrishnan's agony, which he was able to finally overcome, at least at the interview level. Is this insensibility of the university system merely a grammatical one? Or is it a masquerade when faced by challenging and uncomfortable ideas, particularly around the grammar of caste? Muthukrishnan wrote how desperately he had worked to join JNU, 'saving money like [an] ant'.

In another post, Muthukrishnan mentioned the 'invisible, cryptic discrimination' pervading campus life. The oblique nature of this structural violence leaves invisible marks on a Dalit student's body and psyche which no autopsy can reveal. Muthukrishnan's suicide exposed the burden of accumulated structural inequity and prejudice.

Rohith faced a similar sickness in the university, where he

was hounded by the caste politics of Hindutva. It created a radical estrangement with the world. This fever made him break away from it. He was desperate to start a life but the beginning could never take place. The law of caste and untouchability usurps the idea of a free life, and all attempts to break away from it may be devastating. The beginning of freedom is hard to find, or recover, within this 'caste-iron' law that barbs the soul. The beginning in Rohith's case was forever elusive.

If a society, through its educational, social and political structures, practices a discriminatory mindset based on graded inequality—suffocating a university student to the extent that he can imagine the recovery of his equality only in death—the founding principles of such a society need to be dismantled. The founding principles here specifically refer to the logic of caste and the notion of untouchability, based on historically generated territories of exclusion. To live the paranoia of a life of caste (which is antithetical to 'the life of the mind'), to live in the sick fear and revulsion of the shadow of touch, is the surplus humiliation that caste Hindus inflict on themselves. In this country without Rohith Vemula, Muthukrishnan Jeevanathan and other young people like them, the shadow of their death exists, a shadow that demands the abolition of the prejudice and discrimination which made them take their lives and end their possibilities.

～

After Rohith Vemula's suicide, and the growing instances of violence and humiliation faced by Dalits in the last couple of years, it has become an urgent political (and ethical) necessity to reiterate arguments for the annihilation of caste.

Ambedkar's painstaking historical and political critique of the caste system, and the origins of untouchability, was witness to much of his exasperation and anguish. He was concerned about his people and considered every idea which could offer them a different destiny, away from the one forced upon them by Hindu society. In 'Away from the Hindus', Ambedkar writes, 'One way to solve the problem of the Untouchables is for them to abandon Hinduism and be converted to some other religion.' This is a unique prescription-cum-call-to-action, this annihilation-through-conversion, where you propose to a people that they end an oppressive social structure, not by challenging, but by abandoning it. Why abandon? Ambedkar has a precise answer: 'That Hinduism is inconsistent with the self-respect and honour of the Untouchables is the strongest ground which justifies the conversion of the Untouchables to another and nobler faith.'

But Ambedkar's quarrel with Hinduism is not only restricted to the treatment of Untouchables. Gandhi's response to *Annihilation*, which appeared in a series of articles in the *Harijan* (between July and August in 1936), provoked a reply from Ambedkar: 'I am disgusted with Hindus and Hinduism... because I am convinced that they cherish wrong ideals and live a wrong social life.' The language may resemble a moral indictment, but the emphasis is ethical. In 'Away with the Hindus,' Ambedkar writes, 'Historically speaking, service to humanity is quite foreign to Hinduism and to Hindus. The Hindu religion consists primarily, of rituals and observances. It is a religion of temples. Love of man has no place in it.' Ambedkar found a lack of ethical impulses in the Hindu religion and its adherents. He raised the question, '[Does] Hinduism universalize the value of life without distinction?'

The idea of the universal here is not based on a categorical idea, but on an ethical principle of life. It is raised in the context of Hindu society, where life's values are prescribed within caste distinctions. Ambedkar argues for a universal 'principle', where the idea of life can be rid of ascriptive limitations enforced by graded inequality. Everyone should have the equal possibility of touching a free idea of life, an idea free of meanings permanently assigned to one's birth. If an untouchable cannot touch the idea of life that a Brahmin is privileged to, then the society they live in violates the universal principle. Ambedkar was, however, keenly alive to the aspect of difference between individual beings. In *Annihilation*, he made the bold assertion that 'Plato had no perception of the uniqueness of every individual, of his incommensurability with others.' You couldn't 'pigeonhole' individual beings into classes divided according to birth by the chaturvarnya, or the caste system. To be able to live and realize one's incommensurability, is the desirable universal principle Hindu religion falls short of by classifying people into castes.

In 'Away from the Hindus', we come back to the question of the name. By telling the untouchables to get away from the Hindus, Ambedkar also meant, getting 'away from their localities'.

Soumyabrata Choudhury draws our attention to this in his provocative work, *Ambedkar and Other Immortals*. He makes the connection of the name, Antyaja, the original metaphor of exclusion, to that of a place or location. Ambedkar is telling the untouchables here, to dislocate, to change place, to *convert*. Choudhury identifies the subjective aim which Ambedkar has in mind in proposing conversion: it would help untouchables accomplish a 'radical disinterest in Hinduism'. Ambedkar dismisses the option of what he calls 'protective discolouration'. This included people named Chamars calling themselves Ravidas or Jatavas, or people named Dom calling themselves Shilpakars. To give themselves 'other names' within Hindu society doesn't protect untouchables from being *placed* (and fixed) in the caste hierarchy by the sickness of Hindus. The 'other name' within Hindu society would fix the untouchables as *other*. The point was to change this.

Ambedkar equates the idea of conversion to a revolution for the untouchables: 'The name matters and matters a great deal. For, the name can make a revolution in the status of the Untouchables. But the name must be the name of a community outside Hinduism'. The possibility of renaming a whole people could come only from a new community. Ambedkar felt, in order 'to end their isolation the Untouchables must join *another community* which does not recognize caste' (Emphasis added). Joining another community, the untouchables not only gain a new anthropological status, but also a new ethical possibility, of becoming *another*.

Finally converting to Buddhism on 14 October 1956, Ambedkar spelt out his own choice of that other community.

We now go back to a point made earlier, in relation to the prescription Ambedkar makes in *Annihilation*, for the whole Hindu society: 'The names, Brahmin, Kshatriya, Vaishya and Shudra, are names which are associated with a definite and fixed notion in the mind of every Hindu. So long as these names continue, Hindus will continue to think of...hierarchical divisions of high and low, based on birth, and act accordingly. The Hindu must be made to unlearn all this.' How is that possible? Ambedkar offers the same recipe: 'If new notions are to be inculcated in the minds of people, it is necessary to give them new names.' If Ambedkar is asking the untouchables to convert, what lies behind his suggestion for Hindus to discard old names and pick up new ones? In other words, what exactly is Ambedkar asking of Hindus?

Ambedkar, to my understanding, is making two separate points. Regarding untouchables, he is clear that any form of 'clandestine conversion' is not acceptable, as it allows the stigma of untouchability to remain under a new garb. This is not the newness which Ambedkar wished his people to gain in the world. A new destiny bearing a new name requires a new community of relations. A possible name of that community is Buddhism.

What of the Hindus? My contention is that Ambedkar is asking Hindus to undergo a reconversion within the Hindu religion. To discard caste-names, to drop the 'notion' of caste by bringing in, as he put it in *Annihilation*, 'a notional change', Ambedkar wants Hindu society to undergo self-transformation, by an act of self-conversion into *another*. The only way for Hindus to break out of the hierarchical structure of division and exclusion, is to reenter their religion as aliens, renaming themselves. Since Hindu society is the name of a territorialization based on the sanctity of caste, on fixed caste identities, the reconversion into a new world of names will go a long way in annihilating those territories of exclusion. This conversion of Hindu selfhood will not mean merely the change of heart prescribed by Gandhi. But rather, as Ambedkar put it in *Annihilation*, it will be realized 'when inter-dining and inter-marriage have become matters of common course.' To return to the old place as *other*, as the alien it considered others, and begin a fresh encounter without old references (where the names, Brahmin, Kshatriya, Vaishya and Shudra do not exist), is the historical task and responsibility which Ambedkar left Hindus to consider, for their future as an ethical society.

5

The Nation's Bodies

This chapter reflects on ways in which bodies are coerced through mechanisms of control inducted into the lives of citizens, and socio-political violence against marginalized groups. In a massive new drive aimed at tightening the in/security web, the government has made biometric cards mandatory for people to fulfil their obligations as law-abiding citizens. Bodies are being turned into compliant entities of a technological machine that is seemingly abstract but very real—politically and legally. There are other kinds of bodily harm and control faced by people who resist or come in the way of Hindu majoritarianism—mostly, Muslims, Dalits and women. Dalit and Muslim women have suffered public humiliation and barbaric forms of violence, including gangrapes carried out by dominant-caste Hindu men. These men have acted with an alarming sense of entitlement and impunity, often at the instigation of the political class. Lynchings of Dalit and Muslim men by Hindu vigilante gangs intensify newer forms of segregation. The excuse for violence is based on the new ban in many states on cow slaughter and sale, and on propaganda like 'love jihad'.

~

The former attorney general Mukul Rohatgi argued on 2 May 2017, in favour of the unique identity card based on biometric and demographic data, the 'Aadhaar card', to be made mandatory for all Indian citizens. Making his case in the Supreme Court before a bench comprising Justices A.K. Sikri and Ashok Bhushan, Rohatgi made a series of remarks that have since adversely affected citizens' rights. There have been various reports in the media of people denied rations in various parts of the country, because their identity could not be authenticated due to lapses in the data of the Aadhaar-enabled Public Distribution System (AePDS). Hearing the case on 5 April 2018, the Supreme Court censured the government's suggestion that Aadhaar was a panacea for all ills, including bank frauds.

At the hearing on 2 May 2017, invoking Jean-Jacques Rousseau, Rohatgi said that citizens cannot 'live in a vacuum as there is social contract as well. When the state is providing some facility, it is entitled to have your identity.' This distinctly echoes what Foucault explicitly discussed in *The Birth of Biopolitics* regarding the perversion of Rousseau's conception of the 'social contract' since the eighteenth century. To equate 'facility' with 'identity' is to argue that citizens should give up their natural rights for purely utilitarian reasons determined by the government. This compromises the political value of the social contract, suggesting that the citizen trade her rights for securing benefits. In Rousseau's theory of social contract, the idea is based on the legitimacy of the original sovereign—the people—who represent the general or collective will in a democracy. To coerce collective will, asking citizens to comply with the will of the government, is to disregard that contract.

Countering arguments of the petitioners who challenged the government's move, Rohatgi said, 'The arguments on so-called privacy and bodily intrusion are bogus.' To consider privacy and bodily intrusion as bogus is to undermine the basis of the social contract that lies in the moral and natural rights of the citizen. These rights are violated also through capital punishment as much as the extralegal 'encounter killings' by the Indian state.

Rohatgi further asserted, 'One cannot have an absolute right over his or her body.' He added that the 'concept of absolute right over one's body was a myth and there were various laws which put restrictions on such a right.' The right over one's own body is not a matter of degree but of principle. In John Stuart Mill's 'harm principle', power can be legitimately used even against someone's will, to prevent another from being harmed. The instances Rohatgi drew on, of people committing suicide, taking drugs banned by law or tests to check for drunk driving to ensure public safety, corroborate Mill's principle. The social contract aims to secure life, by posing limitations to human freedom. It draws a contentious, often violated line between regulation and coercion by the state.

What if this line is extended in the name of security to significantly blur the distinction between regulation and coercion? Rohatgi's justification for the Aadhaar card was 'as an effective tool to check terror financing and black money.' His larger point on its behalf was, 'An identification system was necessary for an orderly society and to keep pace with technology.' Privacy and bodily intrusion become bogus as ethical issues, but remain a necessary means towards a 'secure' and 'orderly' life for citizens. It is not the citizen's 'absolute right' to her body that seems to be the key issue here but the government's absolute right to compromise the citizen's body in the name of security against terror and corruption. The government wishes to lay claim over your body in order to secure it. 'Parliament is the best judge of the people,' Rohatgi said. As a juridical body of power, the government can exercise a monopoly on what is best for the citizen. This logic of in/security empowers the government to intrude upon the inalienable rights of the democratic subject.

Rohatgi called the Aadhaar card 'an effective tool' to check terror and black money. The visible extension of that vocabulary is the citizen's body as an effective tool to create a network of this large identification system. The body becomes reduced to its exchange value, as the citizen is expected to turn it over to the government in exchange for her security. But aren't we already tools of a network of machines? Haven't we indexed our identity in the many cards we carry? Haven't we already lost our bodies to technology? Rohatgi hit the nail on the head when he asked, 'Can the petitioners today say that they do not have any mobile phone, credit card, driving licence, passport or other identification and they live in the Himalayas?' Since we are already governed by technology, why should the technology of the government which seeks to secure our lives further be a problem?

The problem is not with technology but with government, or with governmental technology. Fundamental political values are at stake when the government seeks to intrude upon natural rights in the name of national security. In arguments based on national security, reality and paranoia merge. If fear aggravates reason in the case of terrorism, black money is a nation's surplus fantasy. The Aadhaar argument transfers the fantasy and fear of the state, into the real lives of people.

The distinction between society and government makes political life possible. Such a distinction is crucial for a democracy. Society is a social and political organization where people have the right to defend their fundamental liberties and demand their rights. It has a critical relationship with government and is free to hold the government accountable for any kind of misrule. Society is the conscience of the government, and ideally limits its powers.

If subjects of natural rights are made to be willing, obedient bodies open to surveillance, they allow a governmental takeover of their diminished, purely biological status. Reduced to a mere specimen in a biometric universe, the citizen shifts from a social to a techno-territorial world. This is how people get transformed into a population, how human life becomes data. It is easier for governments to control populations in the name of security. Despite reservations, the anxiety that they would be denied legal, monetary and other entitlements, have led people to enrol for the Aadhaar scheme. The government has preyed on these fears, coercing citizens to fall in line.

The erasure of the social turns society into government and citizens into governmentalized bodies. This is not Foucault's 'government of oneself', where the citizen, dictated by truth, examines oneself, à la Mahatma Gandhi, and paradoxically starts freely questioning and, at the same time, obeying power. The nationalist citizen today is drugged into being a non-thinking body where obedience is truth. This is an attempt to turn subjects into bodies that don't resist the apparatus of dehumanization. This is not a metaphysical concept but an anthropological condition. There is no self but government. The self has become a managerial entity, a tool that follows and responds to commands, secure and securitized within the technological order of things.

Remember the long queues of compliant citizen-bodies outside ATMs after demonetization was announced on 8 November 2016. A similar phenomenon was visible at the various kiosks used for issuing Aadhaar cards. When people turn into compliant bodies giving up rights for abstract technologies of in/security, they are reduced to bogus citizens. Petitioners who filed complaints against the Aadhaar system and counsels representing them in the Supreme Court, public intellectuals who have voiced their critical opinions in the media, and those protesting in other forums, all offered resistance to this scheme.

The Aadhaar Act has become a legal quagmire. After thirty-eight days of marathon hearings, Attorney General K. Venugopal declared on the conclusive day, 10 May 2018, that the Aadhaar case was the second longest hearing in Indian history. This is testimony to the questions being raised on the ethical, personal and systemic hazards of this identification system. The BJP government, in its hurry to put the biometric web in place, has disregarded citizens' concerns and indulged in legal inconsistencies highlighted by the Supreme Court. On 14 March 2018, the Supreme Court objected to biometric enrolments that have taken place since 2010 under the UPA government, before the law for it (Section 59 of the Aadhaar Act) was passed retrospectively in 2016. Chief Justice Dipak Mishra found the arguments 'badly drafted'.

In an interview regarding the Aadhaar issue, Noam Chomsky emphasized the necessity to ask two different sets of questions: 1) Did the Act come into place 'through democratic participation or public discussion…[which] would lead to a legitimate democratic decision or did it come about simply by an executive order?' 2) Would the Act be used in 'an abusive way to control people' or 'to facilitate people's everyday lives'? Chomsky's distinctions are important, except that he focusses solely on procedural and speculative aspects, leaving out the *political* underpinnings of the government's move. The rights-bearing citizen is fighting for her right to privacy against the mounting political discourse of in/security.

Senior counsel Shyam Divan, who represents the petitioners challenging the Aadhaar Act, said in an opening statement, submitted to court on 17 January 2018, that the central database of the Aadhaar network 'will enable the State to profile citizens, track their movements, assess their habits and silently influence their behavior.' Divan compared the system to a 'switch by which it can cause the civil death of an individual.' The switch is a whimsical metaphor that of the invisible controlling beast marking your territory, and punishing you for crossing it. A Christian petitioner, whose objection was submitted to the Supreme Court in March 2018, found the Aadhaar symbolic of the 'beast' from the Book of Revelation. Revelation 13:16-17 warns of the coming of such a beast, who would ensure 'that no man might buy or sell, save he that had the mark, or the name of the beast, or the number of his name.' Even in a secular exegesis of this allegory the apocalyptic precision of the prediction, regarding the beast still applies. It is the beast of technology. We are today being marked and numbered by such a beast.

~

Farooq Ahmad Dar is a twenty-six-year-old shawl artisan from Chil village in Kashmir. His enthusiasm for asserting his democratic rights literally took a beating on 9 April 2017. The man was among the meagre 7.1 per cent of registered voters who cared to go to a polling booth to cast their vote in the Srinagar by-elections. His terrible story of brutalization has added to the disturbing series of violations in the army-civilian conflict taking place in the Kashmir valley.

The details throw a chilling light on how a sudden rush of suspicion can turn into instant criminalization. Having cast his vote, Dar was on his way to Gampora village in Phulwana district to attend the commemorative ritual of a relative, when he briefly stopped his motorcycle in Utligam village at the sight of some women protestors. This turned out to be his doom, as an army patrol rushed out from an alley right then and caught hold of him. They struck him with rifle butts and wooden sticks without provocation and damaged his bike. The women tried to intervene, but retreated after a warning shot was fired into the air. Dar was not fully in his senses when he was strapped to an army jeep and paraded around many villages for three or four hours.

The video of a beleaguered Dar in pheran and jeans, tied to the jeep's bonnet, and his later narration of the incident, have provoked understandable outrage. Resorting to the war tactic of using a human shield for making a point is a matter of grave concern. Dar remembers people in Khospora village trying to get him released. But the men of the Rashtriya Rifles refused their plea, accusing the man of being a stone-pelter. A white paper was stuck on Dar's chest declaring his crime. In the video we hear a voice announcing in Hindi, 'This is the fate that will befall stone-throwers.' It was a barbaric act by the army, setting an example to warn against against the relentless stone-throwing they face in the valley. A man was turned into a humiliating spectacle, simply because he happened to be in the wrong place. Is the ring devoid of law in the circus of conflict?

The political motivation of a stone-pelter in Kashmir stands opposed to elections. She is not among the believers in Indian democracy. But Dar voted. He possesses his voter slip, serial number 612, as proof. 'I have never ever in my life hurled stones on forces,' Dar said. 'But I am not able to understand why I was beaten ruthlessly and then tied to the vehicle. What was my crime?'

In his words, 'They humiliated me publicly.' Humiliation has come to be an accepted norm in the lives of people who inhabit a risky space, where democracy blurs into a war zone. The soldiers 'played with me like I was a toy,' said Dar. He asked the question, 'Am I a human being or an animal?' To make a human shield of a person dehumanizes the victim by depersonalizing them. A forcibly disabled Dar was reduced to being nonhuman. For those tortuous hours, his body did not belong to him. What happens to the idea of democracy when a man loses his autonomy and is forced to experience animal helplessness? Dar's status as an autonomous subject of democracy collapses in no time into the status of a captive stripped of rights and dignity. Such is the state of exception in Kashmir.

In a widely read and provocative article, Partha Chatterjee traces the 'chilling similarities between the justifications advanced for the actions of the British Indian army in Punjab in 1919 and those being offered today, nearly a century later, in defence of the acts of the Indian army in Kashmir.' Chatterjee called the use of Dar as a human shield by Major Leetul Gogoi, the 'General Dyer moment' in India's postcolonial history. General Bipin Rawat justified the Major making an example of Dar in these words: 'Adversaries must be afraid of you and at the same time your people must be afraid of you. We are a friendly army, but when we are called to restore law and order, people have to be afraid of us.' Dyer, who led his men to indiscriminately shoot at a crowd of 20,000 people in April 1919 at Amritsar's Jallianwala Bagh, said in his defence: 'These were rebels and I must not treat them with gloves on. Yes, throughout the Punjab, I wanted to reduce their moral[e]; the moral[e] of the rebels.'

Rawat's logic, apart from the connection between fear and law, sneaks in the figure of the adversary. Was Dar an adversary? Or did he belong to an adversarial population? If a whole population is considered adversarial, how do we understand phrases like 'friendly army' and 'law and order'? The AFSPA has been in force in Kashmir since July 1990, giving the army extraordinary powers and impunity to tackle a hostile population. Chatterjee is drawing our attention to structural similarities between the Indian army being permanently deployed in regions under the AFSPA, and the presence of armed forces during colonial occupation. What connects a colonial and an occupational army is the legitimacy to spread fear through public spectacle. A people under AFSPA are not understood as people in a democracy, enjoying rule of law, but as a population facing emergency laws. This is the state of exception, where your body is governed by a law that exceeds your rights as a citizen. Dar learnt, to his shock, how an extraordinary law functioning within democracy would suddenly rob him of his own body and treat it as a spectacular tool of martial law and order.

Despite his injury-induced amnesia, Dar recollected names of a few villages he was paraded through: Sonpa, Najan, Chakpora, Hanjiguroo, Khospora, Rawalpora, Arizal and Hardapanzoo. Dar is a brave child of memory in his recounting of places where he witnessed his own humiliation. We know from writers like Primo Levi, W.G. Sebald and Svetlana Alexievich, among others, that memory is the desperate consolation the dehumanized seek to recover their traumatic experience of the world, to stitch back their severed ties with time. Memory fosters coherence. 'There are no bruises over the surface,' Dar said, 'but I am hurt on the inside.' The 'inside' is a place where the spirit of the body resides. Wounding the spirit of the innocent defeats the spirit of democracy. But as Santiago says in Ernest Hemingway's novel, *The Old Man and the Sea*, 'a man can be destroyed but not defeated.' The spirit of a people is more resilient than the temporary destruction of their dreams.

Dar's earlier faith in democracy is questioned by those Kashmiris who see democracy as an empty pretext for forced occupation. His new resolve, however, attests to the growing exasperation in the valley: 'I used to vote but won't do so anymore.'

A year after the outrage provoked by Dar's humiliation, things have taken a turn for the worse. On 5 May 2018, an eighteen-year-old boy, Adil Ahmad Yadoo, who was part of a group of boys at Noorbagh Chowk throwing stones at Central Reserve Police Force personnel, was run over by a police vehicle. In a statement, the police described Yadoo's death as a 'road accident'. A similar incident occurred soon after the government announced a unilateral ceasefire in Kashmir from 17 May, during the fasting month of Ramzan. On 1 June, however, twenty-two-year-old Qaisar Ahmad Bhat, who was part of a stone-throwing demonstration in the Nowhatta locality in Srinagar, was crushed by a CRPF vehicle.

The shrinking distance between the army and stone-pelting Kashmiris has been brought about by the colonization of space by security forces. After stone-pelting incidents intensified, pellet guns or 'non-lethal weapons' were sanctioned in Kashmir in 2010. Since 2016, over a hundred people have suffered severe eye injuries. Space is invaded by a constant fear of harm. Civilians in Kashmir are forced to live under 'spatial schizophrenia', to use Paul Virilio's phrase. Writing about the Palestinian struggle, Virilio called it 'a popular assault, turned suicidal because they have no choice.' There is an echo of this crisis in Kashmir, where Pratap Bhanu Mehta finds a 'deepening death wish'. When the political grounds of life are giving way, when constitutional rights have retreated beyond recognition, people are tempted to risk death. Enclosure of space leads to enclosure of breath. If people cannot breathe, they will challenge the most formidable adversary.

Fascism is not defined by the number of its victims, but by the way it kills them.
—Jean-Paul Sartre, 22 June 1953

Mobs are taking over civic spaces in India. Public lynching, a barbaric form of political expression, seems to have become the new norm in India since the Modi government came to power at the Centre. Lynching is a modern form of ethnic violence, where enemies—differentiated by religion, race, caste or ideology—are brutally eliminated. It is a frightening scenario wherein people turn into government and law at the same time, deciding for themselves who, why and how to kill. It is the rule of sentiments superseding the rule of law. When a community erases the distinction between sentiments and crime, it quickly degenerates into a self-brutalizing society.

Lynching has turned into a vigilante sport in India. On 17 March 2016, two Muslim cattle traders were found hanging from a tree in Jharkhand, allegedly by cattle-protection vigilantes. In July the same year, vigilantes mercilessly beat up seven Dalit men for skinning a dead cow in Una district, Gujarat. Fifty-five-year-old Pehlu Khan, a dairy farmer who was transporting in his truck cattle he had legitimately acquired at a fair, was attacked by dozens of Hindutva vigilantes on 5 April 2017 in Alwar, Rajasthan. The Rajasthan home minister told reporters, 'It is illegal to transport cows, but people ignore it and cow protectors are trying to stop such people from trafficking them.' Since Pehlu Khan, twenty-six cases of violence spawned by cow vigilantism were reported in 2017.

The logic is chilling: those who are lynched are on the wrong side of the law. Those who lynch are seen as protectors of the law. The minister's verdict put all the premises of law to shame. When people sense the government's willingness to provide an alibi for murder, they become emboldened to take the law into their hands. Currently, twenty-four states in India have various regulations prohibiting either the slaughter or sale of cows. The Rajasthan minister's statement is a perfect example validating Ambedkar's point about how the legal and the social apparatus collaborate in enforcing religious customs.

But what does this tell us about the law? Isn't the secular

law of the state, despite the legal restrictions against cow-killing, supposed to protect the citizen from religious gangs? As Martin Luther King Jr. said in his 18 December 1963 address at Western Michigan University, 'It may be true that the law cannot make a man love me but it can keep him from lynching me;' so even though 'morality cannot be legislated, behavior can be regulated.'

But clearly the law has failed Pehlu Khan, Hafiz Junaid, Dileep Saroj, Veshram Sarvaiya and Ramesh Sarvaiya, among countless others. Religion provides no relief either. In *Untouchables or The Children of India's Ghetto*, Ambedkar makes the distinction that unlike slavery, 'that had no foundation in religion,' untouchability is 'primarily based in religion.' He noted that even though 'Roman law declared the slave was not a person,' the 'religion of Rome refused to accept that principle.' But since 'Hindu Law did not regard the Untouchable a person,' he added, 'Hinduism refused to regard him as a human being fit for comradeship.' This distinction, in Ambedkar's opinion, is the reason 'why slavery and serfdom have vanished and why untouchability has not.' The denial of personhood is a key element to lynching. Like the situation in Kashmir, the body of the victim is denied any moral essence, is deprived of rights and easily reduced to an animal.

A conflict between moral law and positive law may ensure the future progress and ethical direction of the latter. But if a group of people are denied a place within the territory of morality, secular sanctions of the state granting them equality before the law are not enough. Ambedkar seems to suggest that it is historically harder to overcome the originary violence of religious law. The denial of moral agency to the untouchable, he feels, prevented Hindu society from developing a sense of 'public' or 'social' conscience. That is why crimes like lynching are carried out with an easy absence of guilt. These crimes committed 'in defence of the social order' are not considered a sin. This makes Ambedkar ask, 'Why does the Hindu indulge in lawlessness in suppressing the untouchables as though such lawlessness is lawful?'

Caste facilitates a culture of prejudice within a system of social law. The 'law of caste', to use Ambedkar's phrase, is a 'law of heredity'. The foundational laws of caste were laid down in the *Manusmriti*, where social rules based on heredity got codified and then assimilated into the Hindu belief system. In time they became customary injunctions, to be differentiated from state laws. Custom, Ambedkar points out, 'is enforced by people far more effectively than law is by the state,' for it is 'the compelling force of an organized people.' Hindu society is stringently organized around these customary laws, which exist with a parallel force in relation to state power. The (social) law born from the shadow of custom keeps the culture of prejudice alive. The law of prejudice haunts the prejudice of law. If cow protection entails the joining of forces between the moral and the state police, the law will simply allow lawlessness in its name. If the law of the state allows the lawlessness of custom to prosper, it is bound to endanger those who lie outside the rule of (majoritarian) sentiments.

Muslims are currently facing similar threats and violence, for being outside the rule of sentiments. In an incident that took place in a Mathura-bound train on 22 June 2017, a sixteen-year-old Muslim boy from Haryana, Hafiz Junaid, was lynched to death, and his three brothers attacked, as they were travelling home from Delhi after shopping for Eid. According to reports, fifteen men wanted four young Muslims to vacate their seats. Upon their refusal, the Muslim boys were abused with communal slurs, accused of being beef-eaters, attacked and thrown off the train as it pulled into a station. It is a dangerous irony when the railways, considered the nation's lifeline, becomes life-threatening for minorities. When fellow passengers suddenly turn into violent mobs, how can people from the minority communities feel safe using public transport? If mere religious differences become a trigger for hate crimes, democracy is in danger.

On 6 December 2017, when India's secular citizens remembered and deplored the demolition of the Babri mosque at Ayodhya twenty-five years ago, a forty-eight-year-old migrant Bengali Muslim labourer, Mohammad Afrazul, was murdered in cold blood in the Rajsamand district of Rajasthan. His murderer was the thirty-eight-year-old Hindu vigilante, Shambhulal Regar. Regar showed an alarming lack of moral scruples, assigning his fourteen-year-old nephew the task of filming the act. In the bone-chilling incident, Regar led Afrazul to a lonely spot in the woods. The victim was led to believe he was going to be offered work. Catching Afrazul unawares, Regar attacked him from behind with a pixie axe. Afrazul pleaded with his assailant in Hindi, 'What happened, sir? Babu, spare my life...' But Regar kept striking remorselessly, till his victim was nearly paralyzed. He then walked towards the camera and ranted, 'This will be the fate of all jihadis. Stop your jihad, or you too will meet this fate.' In another video connected to the crime, Regar revealed his concerns, 'It's my appeal to Hindu sisters, don't fall into the love-trap of these jihadis...These guys, after winning your heart...will keep fulfilling their lust.' He referred to 'jihadis' in the context of 'love jihad'—right-wing propaganda alleging that Muslim men entrap Hindu women into conjugal relations and convert them to Islam. Afrazul's wife, Gulbahar Bibi, said, 'I want justice. He was killed only because he was a Muslim.'

Regar's threat to Muslim men and his appeal to Hindu women assumes that women are gullible and easily manipulated. In Regar's patriarchal mindset, Hindu women need men like him to protect their honour. The self-styled Hindu vigilante will not, however, speak for the women of his community murdered by their own families for choosing even Hindu men of their own accord. Feudal Hindu families don't hesitate to put their daughters to death for exercising their free will to marry a man from a different caste. What goes by the name of protecting a woman's honour is in reality the protection of the family's social status. The patriarchal system that controls the sexual lives and marital choices of Hindu women is based on casteist, Islamophobic and feudal concerns. These concerns feed into the notions of patriarchal pride and dictate its mode of ownership. The honour killings within Hindu society are an obvious extension of the same religious industry of values that keeps Hindu women trapped within the discourse of honour. The 'love jihad' bogey is a move to segregate the Muslim body from all forms of relations with Hindus in the social sphere.

Muslims are today India's new political untouchables. Untouchability, as a practice, emerged primarily from a 'notion' that, as Ambedkar said, produces revulsion. Even though this notion exists only in the mind, it manifests in very real material practices of humiliation and segregation. This notion of untouchability could be (incommensurably) *extended* to talk about the fierce othering of Muslims today, who are faced with a similar pattern of social and political segregation. Ambedkar had specified that the beginning of 'modern untouchability' was 'intimately connected with cow-killing and eating beef.' This injunction also makes Muslims the targets of Hindu religious sanctions in a non-secular environment. The prohibitory decree has extended to conjugal relations with Hindu women. The Hindu nationalist discourse perceives the presence of Muslims as a threat and nuisance to the Hindu body politic.

Coercive methods and violence therefore have become necessary to instil fear. In BJP-ruled Rajasthan, the murder of

Afrazul is the fourth incident of a Muslim being killed on some pretext or another. Nearly thirty Muslims have been lynched all over India since 2015 over suspicions of cow slaughter, and possession and consumption of beef. The 'lawlessness' of the Hindu that Ambedkar complained about, has clearly extended its violent proclivities towards Muslims. Society turning fascist is a deeper moral crisis than the coming of a fascist state. A society can resist a fascist state. How to resist a fascist society?

There is no better answer to this question, other than what is already before us: the love between Ankit Saxena and Shehzadi. The artifice of communally orchestrated segregations has to lose to the incorrigible logic of desire. Though tragically cut short, the love of Ankit and Shehzadi showed resilience and defiance in the face of communal bloodletting. On 3 June 2018, Yashpal Saxena, nearly four months after his son, Ankit, was put to death by Shehzadi's relatives, hosted an iftar party to promote communal harmony. Mr Saxena was reported as saying, 'I thought we should do this as it would be an auspicious start to the trust that I have set up in Ankit's name.' A trust in the name of trust sets a shining example, especially in these untrustworthy times.

~

[A] feminine body is disrespected, but a Dalit feminine body is almost hated.
—Sukirtharani

The Tamil Dalit feminist poet, Sukirtharani, speaking to Divya Karthikeyan, pointed out how 'caste identity and the female body are closely intertwined'. She marks the experiential distinction between Dalit and other women by spelling out the moral imbalance in the response they face as the *other*.

There is an intensification of violence when it comes to the female Dalit body. The upper caste man shares a normative field of values with the upper caste woman. This allows binaries like respect/disrespect or appreciation/ridicule to exist, depending on whether patriarchal norms are being followed. The binaries evaporate in the case of a Dalit woman, for her relation with upper caste society is of pure stigma. There is no scope for any relationship of negotiation, only rejection. The sole law at work here is a law without promise, because it is based on the prejudice of caste and untouchability, a 'notion' unalterable by any other law.

In her report, 'When Shalubai won the chair, but lost the table', writer, translator and Managing Editor of *Pari*, Namita Waikar, writes about Shalubai Kasbe, a forty-four-year-old Dalit woman belonging to the Mang community. When Kasbe was elected sarpanch of Wagholi village in Maharashtra's Osmanabad district in 2011, the young (upper caste) men of the village arbitrarily put a huge bust of Chhatrapati Shivaji on Shalubai's table at the panchayat office. She had to work sitting on a chair without a table for the five years of her tenure.

Waikar writes: 'To sign official panchayat papers—the only symbol of authority conceded to her by the dominant castes—she sat where any other villager would. Across the table from the clerk handling the office registers.'

The official authority of the chair was challenged by turning the table occupied by Shivaji's bust into the symbolic seat of power. The bust of Shivaji became the symbol of cultural (caste) sovereignty. It was used with crude defiance by upper caste villagers to undermine Shalubai's official position. The sovereign appointed by state law was meant to be overshadowed by the sovereign of the social law of caste. It was not simply a playoff between parallel sovereignties. Shalubai's work was disrupted by the bust on her table. They wanted to humiliate her chair. She was forced to shift and share space with her official subordinate. Her authority was structurally displaced from its place, and made to lose its simple prestige. The caste Hindus made Shalubai feel punished for acquiring her new social status.

This is what Guru calls a 'new form of reduction' of a Dalit's 'surplus recognition'. The symbolic order of hierarchy created between table and chair, reflected the *real* social hierarchy existing within and outside the office. The villagers had to resort to this manipulation to reconcile themselves to a Dalit woman in a position of authority.

The hierarchy of caste was thus restored. Shalubai, however, did not leave without leaving her mark. Waikar reports that 'a photograph of Annabhau Sathe, the renowned writer, folk poet and social reformer of the Mang caste, now hangs in the panchayat office.' Shalubai handled the mischief of caste-power that tried to put her social status in place with careful maturity. Shalubai's victory is a historical dent in the casteist distinctions that govern official spaces in India.

But let us pause at the disturbing massacre that took place in Khairlanji village in the Bhandara district of Maharashtra, on 29 September 2006. After Surekha Bhaiyyalal Bhotmange, a Dalit woman, lodged a police complaint against people belonging to the dominant Kunbi caste over a land dispute, Surekha, her daughter Priyanka and her two sons were paraded naked in the village, sexually assaulted, and hacked to death.

The judge in the Nagpur High Court concluded that this was a case of revenge killing and not a caste atrocity.* Are the two mutually exclusive? Clearly, caste colours the revenge in this crime, which is enacted on the body of

---

*'Khairlanji case: HC commutes death sentence for six', *The Hindu* (July 15, 2010). https://www.thehindu.com/news/national/Khairlanji-case-HC-commutes-death-sentence-for-six/article16196520.ece

the victims, and transfigures the sexual humiliation into a hierarchically determined feeling of hate, ultimately leading to murder. Humiliation is also a way to demonstrate what is in store for Dalits, if they dare to make legal complaints against unauthorized shows of power by the upper castes. Dalit bodies are an extension of the land they barely possess. They can be violently dispossessed of both land and body at the will of the upper castes. The act of killing is a sovereign act of limitless caste power, where the life of the untouchable is shown its limits. This violence in Hindu society is sanctioned by the law of caste, which enables perpetrators to completely strip the victims of every layer of dignity, before killing them.

Such stark episodes corroborate Sukirtharani's distinction between disrespect and hate. In case of the female Dalit body, humiliation becomes the *necessary* exception for upper caste men, and serves the norm of vengeance. The Dalit woman demanding her rights to her own land, was seen as a political transgression of her social status. Her complaint to the police was an act of faith in state law. That faith was violently crushed by the intervention of caste law, proving which law reigns supreme. It was enough to kill a Dalit man for such a transgression, but in the case of the Dalit woman, even her despised body is sexualized in the act of upper-caste vengeance. As the instrument of her daring and violation of the caste law, it is punished with sexual humiliation.

In the interview, Sukirtharani speaks of the general problem of ownership, and what it denies women: 'The female body is never allowed to be in solitude, it is always defined by the man who possesses it, who makes love to it, or by whom it was born to.' Solitude is understood ethically here. It is seen as a space and a condition, where it is possible to be with oneself, alone. Solitude allows one to have conversations with oneself. If this solitude is disallowed, interrupted or violated, the body is robbed, not only of its individual autonomy, its historical and political agency (identified in first-person by the 'I' or the 'me') but also of its ethical possibility, its 'you'. The body is something more than just itself, *more* than the contours of self-centric understanding and the determination of the autonomous and agential self. The double-ness of the body is a forked root of desire, of the desiring body.

It is tragic when this conversation is violated and conditioned by a moral binary of pure/impure, as Sukirtharani points out: 'A woman's body is being portrayed as a sacred thing, as a synonym of purity. I call this body-politics.' This is a religious injunction on the body, codifying the body's limits, its 'lakshman-rekha', territorializing its space and scope, and worse, instituting a patriarchal judge who takes charge and assigns its roles. As Pandita Ramabai Sarasvati put it, 'The priesthood (Brahman caste) were appointed to be the spiritual governors over all.' The governor of the soul is also the governor of the body. A woman cannot lay claim to her body without challenging the appointment of the government of the soul.

We know from Foucault that the apparatus of power, to control and regulate women's sexuality, uses methods of examining, disciplining and punishing the body. This closely resembles what Sukirtharani refers to as 'body-politics'. Since the soul is considered pure and the body impure in comparison, and in constant need of purification in order to come close to or resemble the soul, it is trapped in two possibilities—either of endlessly purifying itself, or being endlessly tempted to render itself impure. Foucault writes in *Discipline & Punish*: 'The soul is the effect and instrument of a political anatomy; the soul is the prison of the body.' This is the politics of the sacred, where sexuality is considered a surplus to be tamed in the name of a spiritual economy. It is this very surplus that gets violated in encounters where woman faces the brunt of territorial violence. Her body is pitted against the territorializing machine that works either in the name of a caste law, or a communal law, or both.

The Muslim woman faces a violence born of another economy of violent segregation, one that follows from the history and memory of Partition. Akhila Ashokan, a twenty-four-year-old homeopathy student from the Kottayam district of Kerala, caused a nationwide stir when she converted to Islam, renamed herself Hadiya, and married the twenty-seven-year-old Shafin Jahan. Hadiya's father, K.M. Ashokan, had taken the matter to the Kerala High Court, insinuating Jahan was an ISIS agent. After the court annulled his marriage, Jahan had to move the Supreme Court to get back together with his wife. The apex court directed the National Investigation Agency (NIA) to investigate the allegations. But the real controversy was political, since Hadiya had challenged the Hindu Right's conspiracy theory of 'love jihad'.

Hadiya's consistent affirmation of her voluntary conversion and marriage cut no ice with people. Even though she managed to convince the Supreme Court of her free will and consent regarding her conversion and marriage, the disturbing aspect of this case is that it has become increasingly difficult for Hindu women to defend their relationships with Muslim men. In the Supreme Court hearing of the case in November 2017, Hadiya conveyed her exasperation at her ten months of confinement, which included six months with the family. Her answers to two questions are worth pausing over:

> Court: What are your dreams for the future?
> Hadiya: I want to be free [In Malayalam, 'swathanthryam']...
> Court:...Who do you want as your guardian?

Hadiya: My husband. I want someone who accepts me as Hadiya.*

If the court expected Hadiya to offer her dreams for the future in calculable terms, it was disappointed. Hadiya named freedom, something beyond measure, beyond everything that was measuring and controlling her, denying her the life she had chosen freely, of her own will. To the next question, Hadiya's reply is equally exemplary. She radically alters the conventional meaning of a guardian who is appointed as protector and provider. Hadiya understands a guardian to be someone very different from a legal appointee, someone who won't police her will to be herself, her name and her faith. She rejects the patriarch and the government in one stroke. Hadiya wants to make peace, expecting the system to leave her alone. On 8 March 2018, the Supreme Court restored Hadiya's marriage, cancelling the Kerala High Court order. It however allowed the NIA's investigation of her husband to continue.

After the Supreme Court freed Hadiya from her parents' custody in November 2017, the Chief Justice had asked her if she wanted the state to bear the expenses of her education. She declined the offer. The state was keen to see Hadiya as its moral property. She wanted to be free from the gaze of the state, and be allowed to lead her life freely, in her husband's care. Freedom is the best argument against being property.

There are women who fare much worse, when thrown into the vortex of territorial politics. Neha Dixit's report, 'Shadow Lines', is an account of rape survivors in the Jat-Muslim riot that took place on 7 September 2013 in Uttar Pradesh. It all

---

*'Hadiya's Case: What Happened in Court Hall No. 1 of the Supreme Court,' *The NEWS Minute* (November 28, 2017). https://www.thenewsminute.com/article/hadiya-s-case-what-happened-court-hall-no-1-supreme-court-72325

started with unconfirmed news of a Muslim boy in Kawal village eve-teasing a Jat girl around the end of August. Dixit estimates from conversations in relief camps that hundreds of Muslims were killed, almost a hundred women raped and a lakh displaced. The report claims that several Hindu khap panchayats (who are known to instigate honour killings) twenty kilometres outside of Muzaffarnagar to declare a war against 'love jihad'. The narratives of the women are numbing.

I shall only mention two Muslim women. One named S, in her mid-30s, had questions: 'Why were we raped if a boy eve-teased a girl? Did the whole nation go about raping the women of the community of Nirbhaya's rapists to avenge what was done to her?' The bewilderment is heartbreaking. The question she raises is political. S has learnt that the nation is not on her side. Her body is without a nation.

Another forty-year-old Muslim woman, named Sb, narrated her story: 'They inserted a big stick into me, and I started bleeding. They revelled in the sight of my blood, then raped me.' Rape as a hate crime is an act of violence on a despised body. It marks the crossing of a boundary, an outer limit of a territory we call humanity (all territories are human and designate everyone outside them as other). Women outside of this territory are rendered not-human, as mere property. This coercive and limiting law of property which treats women customarily as private property is justified in the name of sacred as well as territorial law. All territory is sacred, and the sacred is territorial. This law is barely ever concealed by what claims to historically substitute it: the secular law of the liberal-democratic state.

Men, as beasts of territory, are not subject to ethical laws. Any transgression of the male order provokes violence, because men cannot allow the transgression of their own law. The acts of humiliation against women spring from a fear (natural, historical) of being provoked into losing their ties with territoriality (marked by caste, religion, race, nation), the fear of becoming *another*. In opposition to this fear, the courage—of the Muslim women near Muzaffarnagar, the courage of Hadiya, the courage of Irom Sharmila who fasted for eleven years, and defended her relationship with a British-Indian man, saying 'I am not a goddess. I want to be a human being,' and the courage of Shalubai, who kept her chair after being robbed of her table—shows us that there are people looking for another idea of being, of being *another*... unmarked by the territorialities of oppression.

The Wikipedia page titled 'Disappearance of Najeeb Ahmed' has the introductory line, 'Najeeb Ahmed is a missing first year MSc Biotechnology student of Jawaharlal Nehru University, in New Delhi, India, who has been missing under suspicious circumstances since 15 October 2016.' The story of Ahmed's altercation with students belonging to the ABVP, has taken several shapes and forms. He has been declared an 'accused' by the administration. Fellow students insist he is the victim, giving details of how he was badly beaten by a group of students despite the presence of authorities. Strangely, there is no verifiable account of his disappearance. His mother, Fatima Nafees, faced detention after she was dragged away by the police for protesting the state's inaction over her son's disappearance. 'Where is my son?' she asked in return and, often breaking down, she has been asking ever since.

A nine-player football team from JNU, named 'Red Star JNU', played in the Capital Carnival tournament on November 6, wearing jerseys with 'Najeeb' written on them. Predominantly Malayalis, the team said they had cancelled their Onam programme on October 22 as everyone was depressed about Ahmed's disappearance. Najeeb's disappearance has raised a series of ironies and questions, besides exposing the obvious risk faced by students belonging to the minority communities, even in elite academic institutions.

Najeeb is a disembodied name, looking for its body. Najeeb is looking for Najeeb. The nation doesn't know where Najeeb is to be found. How come the long arm of the law falls short of finding Najeeb? Or is that arm being obstructed from finding him? Is something sacred being protected by Najeeb's disappearance? Is Najeeb a threat to what is sacred? Is the sacred a secret law of the majority that runs the nation? Is Najeeb the name of a secular law that profanes the sacred? Are Muslims profane, Hindus sacred? Does the disappearance of a Muslim boy hold back something we are all supposed to know, or suspect, or challenge, or be scared of? Does Najeeb not unsettle the nation's 'collective conscience'? Does the 'collective' stand for 'majoritarian'? Does the majority stand for justice only when it is out for revenge? Is the nation fine with Najeeb's disappearance, seeing justice in *his very disappearance*?

Is Najeeb's disappearance the nation's revenge against its minorities? Is the nation always threatened by everything minor, a revenge-seeking majoritarian machine against the minor? This is what Arjun Appadurai calls the nation's 'fear of small numbers'. He traces these fears to two sources: a notion of national 'purity', and a perception of 'small numbers' as having real potential to disrupt the nation's security. The latter is used to legitimize the former mindset, where the nation defines its borders of purity by stigmatizing certain people. The constant accusation against a minority community of harbouring terrorists is a deliberate ploy to marginalize it.

Are all such disappearances a secret technique and a cruel method of retribution?

Nothing about the missing student's life is verifiable, or believable any longer. Truth is a pending court case waiting for the victim to appear. But the victim infinitely postpones his arrival, and expectations run thin. The police are as clueless as children about the boy's disappearance. In Kafka's *The Castle*, K is told, 'We have a saying here that you may be familiar with: official decisions are as shy as young girls.' In Najeeb's case, there is official reluctance towards being decisive, as the police remain shy about finding Najeeb, alive or dead. Is that the reason for the delay? That he may be found dead rather than alive, immediately implicating those who beat him up? As long as Najeeb's body isn't found, lies can roam, rumours can breed, and speculations can prevail. Najeeb is the mysteriously missing (minor) organ of India's body politic. He is not alone. There are many young men like him, missing within India's borders, in Kashmir, in Manipur. The organs of the state are silent. Is the state looking to find them, or looking to lose them (for us) further? There is a secret link, we know, between the law of disappearance and the disappearance of law. This is what we know as the secret law, not simply of the secular state, but of its customary counterpart, the sacred law of the nation, where the politics of majoritarianism prospers.

6
Thinking Against Power

This chapter looks at how power, by its very nature, provokes what opposes it, what we call thinking. Thinking, in its political and intellectual sense, denotes an activity that is aware of power, and what it does to the world and to life. It has been a subject of debate among many thinkers. We enter the debate between Ambedkar and Gandhi, and bring in Frantz Fanon to think about how the violence of power limits our moral and ethical choices, and responses. And yet, is it possible to resist power by means other than violence? Is thinking against power enough to haunt power? The problem of a new brand of nationalism facing universities in India, gives us the context to rethink these questions. The resistances against nationalism, caste and other embedded patriarchies, help us imagine the political task of our times.

~

I am that gadfly which God has attached to the state…You will not easily find another like me.

—Plato, *The Apology of Socrates*

'I think, therefore I am,' said Descartes famously. What makes people think? Throughout the history of the world, people have continued to think, even under oppression. It is thinking against oppression that has brought new ideas into the world. Even the idea of history itself, from being the story of emperors and their conquests, now includes the story of people's struggles against conquests and emperors. Socrates, whom Plato refers to as the 'gadfly' of Athens, had infuriated its authorities for praising their arch-rival, Sparta. In our times, if an intellectual from Delhi praises Lahore, it will be considered a similar offence.

For raising questions regarding the system of Athenian justice, Socrates was, ironically, put to death. The accusation that he was corrupting the youth was a cover-up for the fear of a man who could think. Galileo, among many others, was charged with heresy by the church in the medieval era, when he made discoveries contrary to religious beliefs. In twentieth-century Rome, thirty-five-year-old Antonio Gramsci was imprisoned and sent to a camp for his opposition to Mussolini. At his trial, the Fascist prosecutor said, referring to the Marxist theoretician, 'We must prevent this brain from functioning for 20 years.'

To think itself is to resist the designs of power. And that scares power, for it is paranoid about resistance. Power can be understood as a narcissist, who is alarmed by the possibility of anyone disturbing her reflection in the water. A person's thinking can be a ripple that disfigures power's own reflection, causing it to tremble in rage or anxiety.

The Finnish poet and aphorist, Paavo Haavikko, said, 'Real delicacies are raw: oysters, salmon, and power.' He meant to say that, like oysters and salmon, power tastes best when served *naturally*. The nature of power is its raw temptation of violence, its temptation of raw violence. Power, by its nature, will always prevent new thought, for the latter will threaten its existence. All power can do in terms of novelty, as witnessed in history, is devise newer methods of coercion. The state does not merely invent newer technologies of torture, but newer laws, to prevent people from expressing themselves and questioning the excesses of power.

As a nation, we have faced both during the anti-colonial struggle. Gandhi's Dandi March in 1930, a nonviolent, civil disobedience movement to protest the salt tax enforced by the colonial government, was not merely a form of political protest. It was a method of resistance that Gandhi, the gadfly who irritated the British Empire, developed by thinking about nonviolence. It was a unique method to challenge power, without using violence. If violence becomes a part of a movement of resistance, it allows power to respond with the superior force it has at its disposal. Power has no qualms about using an unequal measure of violence to meet any violent resistance against it. Such resistance movements, which use violence as retaliation, are at a real risk of elimination. Gandhi's method of challenging power by not only avoiding violence, but developing a whole new language of nonviolent protest, caused immense moral and political discomfort for British rulers.

By thinking nonviolently, Gandhi opened up radical spaces for protesting against the colonial government and its machinery. Such thinking is possible only when a certain space for nonviolence exists, when resistance takes on the quality of the power it is resisting. Gandhi's resistance gains meaning and force only because it refused to respond to the colonial regime in its language of violence. Violent retaliation to violence may seem logical, but the danger with logical thinking is that it is hugely invested in naturalism. By claiming that it is only natural to respond to violence with violence, one loses moral and ethical ground against the violence of power. To argue that violence is natural is to say that human beings are naturally violent. But it is power that is constructed on the idea of violence. It is possible to critique it only because human beings have ethical possibilities, which are opposed to this naturalist justification of power. To argue that human beings are naturally violent pushes the idea of justice into a naturalist realm, where violence takes on a just mantel. This argument quickly relapses into the 'logic' of an eye-for-an-eye and a tooth-for-a-tooth. It is against such logical end games that thinking comes operates.

Thinking breaks into the 'logic' of violence by asking questions of it. Gandhi's satyagraha is a movement of thinking translated into practice, which asked questions of the colonial regime—questions of truth, community and freedom. If we go by the ethically challenging assumption that all power is ultimately illegitimate, then all thinking against power is equally legitimate. In such a view, thinking itself is an ethical act, for it raises questions regarding the legitimacy of power, which is inherently violent, and hence, unethical.

When Ambedkar challenged Gandhi before being coerced into the Poona Pact of 1932, he too raised a question against what he thought was Gandhi's unjust method of co-opting the untouchables. Gandhi's response to Ambedkar's challenge was to go on a fast unto death. Gandhi's method of nonviolence—Ambedkar called it 'blackmail'—faced its limits before the latter's challenge. But does thinking break down in this moment of political confrontation between Ambedkar and Gandhi? Not at all. For in the case of both Gandhi and Ambedkar, the act of thinking is to push the boundaries of belief.

The belief systems of the social, cultural and religious world, for the sake of perpetuating itself, may resort to violence, like power. Thinking against power, hence, is also thinking against beliefs, and thus, both naturally come into conflict. Gandhi was challenging Hindu beliefs as much as people's belief in the idea of violence, by fasting against the proposal of separate electorates for untouchables. Ambedkar challenged Gandhi's views on this issue, and took the debate further. Unlike a violent face-off, the encounter between Gandhi and Ambedkar opened up questions regarding the limits of the nonviolent method, and its morally coercive tactics. To Gandhi's credit however, his method allows us to challenge him, raise questions, and think against the limits of his nonviolent resistance. This debate is alive even today, irrespective of whether or not Gandhi was justified in using the threat of self-annihilation.

Even if one does not side with Ambedkar on this issue, it may be admitted that Gandhi's action, ironically, elevates Ambedkar's position, as Gandhi's gesture borders on coercion, playing a politics of life and death. But because Gandhi suffers for it as much as he forces Ambedkar to suffer, a space is created for us to think about the limits and possibilities of such a politics. This is why the Ambedkar-Gandhi encounter is one of the most fascinating political debates in modern history. The two men publicly resisted each other with their demands, and engaged with each other's ideas without resorting to violence. These were two political leaders with their own sense of intellectual honesty and clarity, who took each other's words thoughtfully and responded sincerely. Despite Ambedkar's fierce attacks on Hindu dharma, a religion which Gandhi critiqued but was not prepared to dismiss, he acknowledges Ambedkar in his response to *Annihilation*, as 'uncompromising', among the 'ablest', and 'most irreconcilable'. Ambedkar agrees 'with every word' regarding Gandhi's point that 'a religion has to be judged not by its worst specimens but by the best it might have produced.' And yet, Ambedkar goes on to refute even that contention as an insufficient defence. These debates in the public sphere by two popular political figures were not restricted to party lines or measured by narrow strategic advantages. They were part of a *movement*. The politics of our times is a politics without the movement, and no longer thinks.

Only open, thinking encounters can create questions and debates. Godse shooting Gandhi was a closed and violent encounter that helped no debate, unless one cares to justify murder. To justify murder requires no thinking. All it needs is belief. After nearly seventy years of independence, we are again faced with the old questions. India is a democracy today, and by definition, this means a state and mode of government which allows thinking and dissent. But suddenly, there seems to be a dangerous consensus that thinking which goes against power is seditious.

During the anti-colonial struggle, nationalism made people think about ways to oppose colonial injustice. Today, nationalism is asking people to play the opposite role: it is preventing people from thinking about justice. Is the new political definition of nationalism based on an assumption of consensual coercion, where thinking is disallowed? Is nationalism a celebration of the narcissistic, logical and naturalist construct of power instead of the critical, ethical and liberating idea that once inspired Gandhi and Ambedkar?

Criticism is a form of nation-love which allows thinking and dissent against power, for power itself is far from delivering justice. The only moral legitimacy which the state has, comes from its pledge to impart justice. That is why we believe in the law. Ironically, however, some of our laws are still dragging on from the colonial era, and even logically, we can see that they are of no help. They are as opposed to delivering justice now, as they were then.

How can the most logical of nationalist love and pride accept such a thing? In his famous lecture 'What is Called Thinking?', the German philosopher, Martin Heidegger, says that memory 'is the gatherer of thought'. We are given the ability to think through memory, as it opens up the space for us to remember. The Indian nation was born out of the ripped belly of Partition. The impossibility of reconciling with that moment leads nationalists to get caught in the pathological obsession to correct the past, by constructing fantasies and not acknowledging the histories of *internal* injustice. To contemplate the past, besides criticism, we need a thinking that helps expand the past which is forever moving back in time. Memory gathers thought by recollecting lost time, where the secrets of our fears, intimacies and prejudices lie. In the words of Milan Kundera, the 'struggle of man against power is the struggle of memory against forgetting'. If our historical memory is the source of nationalist violence, we must ponder over a simple fact: what memories (about our past) have we given up, in order to be left with only violence? In other words, what have we *forgotten* of our history, which once made us think, but today only makes us want to destroy each other? Not just gadflies, but all of us need to ponder this question.

~

It will be interesting to open up the Ambedkar-Gandhi debate to include Frantz Fanon, the Martinician psychiatrist and thinker, specifically regarding the question of truth and violence in relation to power. All three thinkers wrote in the context of the anti-colonial struggle.

For Ambedkar and Gandhi, the relationship between truth and violence is understood in relation to ahimsa. For Fanon, the question is a double-edged sword, as colonialism operates under the deep shadow of racism. For Ambedkar, resisting colonial violence is a complex battle, since apart from the united, nationalist struggle, the question of caste has to be posed internally, within the society struggling against colonialism. Gandhi places the nonviolent satyagrahi against all sovereign power by claiming that '[it] is a fundamental problem of satyagraha that the tyrant, whom the satyagrahi seeks to resist, has power over his body and material possessions, but he can have no power over his soul.' It is soul-force or truth-force that Gandhi's satyagrahi uses as a political weapon against the violent power of the colonizer.

In contrast, Fanon approaches the question of violence in *The Wretched of the Earth* by first clarifying the relationship between truth and nationalism:

> The problem of truth ought also to be considered. In every age, among the people, truth is the property of the national cause. No absolute verity, no discourse of the purity of the soul can shake this position...Truth is that which hurries on the break-up of the colonialist regime; it is that which protects the natives, and ruins the foreigners. In this colonial context there is no truthful behavior.

For Fanon, it is impossible to expect any truthful behaviour under the colonialist regime, because the only truth at stake is a complete break with the colonial regime. Truth, for Fanon, is as much a matter of dignity and point of difference vis-à-vis the colonizers as it is for Gandhi, but there is a more fundamental difference here. For Fanon, the property of truth is intrinsically linked to nationalism while for Gandhi it is also linked to a critique of nationalism. Truth, for Gandhi, lay in the nonviolent establishment of justice, which cannot be achieved by the violence of nationalism. For Fanon, politics is what is at stake vis-à-vis truth, for truth is an event of freedom which can be realized through political victory. For Gandhi, it is the opposite: truth is what is at stake vis-à-vis politics. Gandhi perceives truth as something that is not wholly understood or explained through politics, but it nevertheless is an ethical activity within politics. Gandhi holds politics to be *necessary*: it is the necessary condition for truth in modern times. The point however is not to lose sight of truth in politics. Truth is Gandhi's benchmark for politics.

Fanon also deviates from Gandhi's 'spiritual' soul-body distinction in terms of the effects of colonialism. For Fanon, the colonized 'owes the fact of his very existence, that is to say his property, to the colonial system.' He formulates an existential meaning for the colonized subject—there is no property of the subject outside colonialism. For Gandhi, the soul is a property which can resist the influence of the colonizer.

Ambedkar presents a fascinating contrast to both Gandhi and Fanon. To begin with, he agrees with Fanon about the question of truth in relation to oppressive regimes like colonialism or the caste system. Truth is the discourse of Brahminical power, and its edifice needs to be smashed. Under the stain of the caste system, the upper caste cannot behave truthfully, nor will they tolerate any truthful behaviour from the people they oppress. In his reply to Gandhi's response to his undelivered lecture on the annihilation of caste, Ambedkar writes with polemical force, '[as] a Mahatma he may be trying to spiritualise Politics. Whether he has succeeded in it or not, Politics have certainly commercialised him. A politician must know that Society cannot bear the whole truth and that he must not speak the whole truth; if he is speaking the whole truth it is bad for his politics.'

What is the 'whole truth' that Gandhi is hiding in order to oppose the call for annihilating caste? Ambedkar says that, '[the] reason why the Mahatma is always supporting Caste and Varna is because he is afraid that if he opposed them he will lose his place in politics.' By not attacking the foundations of caste, Gandhi is seen as deviating from his own truth-claim. Ambedkar finds an irreconcilable dichotomy in the two roles Gandhi plays: that of a saint and a politician. The politician does not allow the saint to be wholly truthful. For Ambedkar, Gandhi's politics does not fully acknowledge his responsibilities as a saintly man who proclaims to speak the truth. He reminds us that saints have never campaigned against caste and untouchability. So, as he puts it, 'dependence on saints cannot lead us to know the truth.'

For both Fanon and Ambedkar, truth can only be grasped in opposition to power. It is only in the destruction of the racist, colonial regime or the Brahminical law of exclusion that truth shows forth.

For Fanon, since the racist regime perpetrates violence upon the body of the native, the problem reveals itself in this manner:

> The violence of the colonial regime and the counter-violence of the native balance each other and respond to each other in an extraordinary reciprocal homogeneity…The development of violence among the colonised people will be proportionate to the violence exercised by the threatened colonial regime.

Since Fanon's schema of thought has no place for human beings who can be saved from the racist colonizer's violence, he is caught in the equalization of violence. The counter-violence of the native is nothing more than the violence that has been put into him by the colonizer. Racist colonialism creates a situation where violence is natural; it enhances a naturalist propensity for violence, and the native is trapped in this logic. Concerning violence, it is a 'no-exit' situation for Fanon.

Ambedkar might agree with Fanon that the Brahminical system, as much as the colonial, introduces a violence into the encounter with the oppressed. But Ambedkar is also invested in the Buddhist idea of ahimsa, which makes a distinction between 'the will to kill' and 'the need to kill'. He contends that the Brahminical caste system 'has in it the will to kill.' The perpetuation of power and self-interest is what drives this will to commit violence. Further, this 'will to kill' is bolstered by certain 'concrete preliminary conditions' in the form of the foundational laws of caste, as given in the *Manusmriti*.

For Ambedkar, the distinction between 'will' and 'need', or the desire for positive harm and unavoidable compulsion, is necessary. However, the necessity of violence is left to the individual: 'No doubt [the Buddha] leaves it to every individual to *decide* whether the need to kill is there. But with whom else could it be left? Man has Pradnya, and he must use it.' Ambedkar's formulation opens up a new possibility which exists *prior to* the moment of decision. It is an ethical decision: whether or not to kill, or, if there is a need to kill. The 'will to kill' is a conscious, rational decision to harm, and the 'need to kill' asks one to pause and consider the ethical consequence of their action. The 'need to kill' is closer to the vulnerability of life in its withholding of the violent impulse.

The other interesting distinction within nonviolence, which Ambedkar pays attention to, is between nonviolence as a 'Principle and as a Rule'. According to him, the Buddha 'did not make Ahimsa a matter of Rule' but a 'matter of Principle'. As he understands it, 'A principle leaves you freedom to act. A rule does not. Rule either breaks you or you break the rule.' This is slightly different from Gandhi's version of nonviolence: for him, ahimsa is a concept and a conduct where the principle becomes the rule. Since Ambedkar believed in 'absolute nonviolence' in opposition to social violence, and not simply violence at the individual level, he would find Gandhi's idea of ahimsa lacking as a social ethic. Gandhi's ahimsa leaves the question of relative violence unanswered. In contrast to the centrality of 'self' in Gandhi's politics, Ambedkar emphasized 'caste' as the cardinal category for understanding Hindu identity and Indian history. If truth, for Gandhi, was outside the traps of (modern) history, in a past idyll of community life, for Ambedkar that truth included the annihilation of untouchability.

Power provides the ground for (political) thinking, and sets its limits. Violence enables Gandhi to think, and keeps him focussed on how to tackle that question. Caste and untouchability does the same for Ambedkar, as colonial racism does for Fanon. Gandhi transforms the idea of power that we confront outside us, by situating it within. Through this manoeuvre, he tries to establish the idea of self-sovereignty. For Ambedkar, caste and untouchability do violence to the body, and it is necessary to annihilate the very system of thinking which produces it. In Ambedkar's anti-systemic thinking, people convert themselves into a just and fraternal future. For Gandhi, thinking is the recovery of a truth lost in the corrupt deviations of modernity, and politics is a way to heal people back into a just relationship. Fanon finds no respite from the constricting grip of racist power, except by tearing oneself from that violence through un-Gandhian self-sacrifice. Between them, we learn three historic tendencies in thinking politics during the time of colonialism.

~

(I)t is my conviction that my countrymen will gain truly their India by fighting against that education which teaches them that a country is greater than the ideals of humanity.

—Rabindranath Tagore,
'Nationalism in India', 1917

India is proud of its argumentative tradition. But that culture of debate and tolerance has been increasingly under attack since the BJP regime took charge in 2014. In February 2017, Ramjas College in Delhi University arranged a seminar on nationalism, free speech, dissent and sedition. As panelists discussed India's caste system, a mob of hundreds from the ABVP, a right-wing students' party, surrounded the college. The ABVP had earlier objected to the inclusion of Umar Khalid by the organizers of the seminar. Khalid had attained prominence in February

2016 after being arrested, along with other student leaders, in connection to a meeting organized by former members of the Democratic Students Union (DSU), a left-wing group, protesting the killing of Afzal Guru and Maqbool Bhat. The organizers of the seminar in Delhi University agreed to drop Khalid as a speaker. Nonetheless, the mob charged the auditorium: hurling rocks, breaking windows, and cutting off electricity. Scores of professors and students were trapped as the bricks and stones rained down, and the police stood by watching. The seminar was called off. The day after the cancelled seminar, DU students and teachers conducted a silent march to protest this attack on free speech. Marchers were seriously hurt when students and other members of various Hindu Right groups attacked them. The police once again played spectator.

Another incident occurred in February 2016 at Jai Narain Vyas University in Jodhpur, in the northern state of Rajasthan, when some students were angered by a visiting feminist professor, Nivedita Menon, criticizing India's policies in Kashmir and playing with the image of the Indian map by displaying it upside down (as any map would look from space). Her demonstration was inspired by an editorial in *Himal Southasian* (14 March 2016) which used a 'right-side-up' map of the region. Menon's demonstration that idolatry of a map is simply a matter of spatial perspective and that a map is unlike a flag, provoked intimidation instead of discussion. As if thinking itself is anti-national. The students, angry at the perceived disrespect to India, forced the event to a close. Rajshree Ranawat, the assistant professor in the English department who had invited the speaker, had to flee town for several days, fearing for her life. On her return, she discovered that the university had suspended her. In May 2017, a Bench in the capital's high court pulled up the city police for its inaction when a woman dean of Delhi University, Ved Kumari, who was had earlier been abused and threatened by ABVP activists, was again held hostage in her office by students. The admonition had a Biblical ring to it: 'You have thrown her to wolves. You are feeding wolves by not separating them from the sheep.' Nationalism is a Darwinian force that makes the law favour the wolves, causing constant fear and death among the sheep.

The future is born from debating ideas. India's universities and colleges have long been dominated by left and liberal ideas. The Hindu nationalists are now attempting a hostile takeover. The Indian Left is also guilty of using coercion and aggressive propaganda to keep other political ideas at bay in some universities of Kerala and West Bengal. They ignore and discredit other political discourses, including Ambedkarite thought. Regarding this, Choudhury raises the provocative question: 'It is more or less settled that the Left has no new arrow to shoot—but is it within their capacity to *receive* a new Ambedkarite wound?' There is no thinking without wounding, particularly if you have neglected a wound beside you, the wound of the other. Thinking is born from the other, and the university offers the first chance for it. To *think* politics means raising new questions about old certainties. Universities are meant to encourage and perform that critical task. Replacing debate with violence in the name of nationalism kills democracy and the possibility of a just future.

A university is not supposed to be the mirror image of the community ('parivar') you belong to. It is, by definition and ethos, a community at odds with your sentimental ties to the world—a place where you meet people of diverse backgrounds and ideologies, and learn to deal with your differences, political and otherwise. To accept and respect those differences, even as you try to bridge or reject them, are the choices at hand.

A university is a place where students learn to resist all that is forced upon them, all that does not taste like liberty. Resistance to power is the responsibility of university education. The 'Pinjra Tod' (Break the Locks) movement in 2015, when women demanded relaxation of the outrageous restrictions on their mobility and freedom, challenged the inherent gender bias in the policing of young students. The movement started in the university spaces of Delhi and spread to other towns and cities. It is a unique resistance movement, an amorphous collective without leaders.

Only resistance is truly universal. A university is also a place where you put forward your best political argument for a cause and measure it against the arguments of others. It is, by extension, no place for scuttling ideas by appealing to primal and regressive instincts like murder.

Violence is not an idea, though it may serve an idea. Nationalism is an idea which does not serve any idea other than itself. In this climate of hyper-nationalism, our cultural and intellectual worlds stand divided into antagonistic zones where the sole question of any importance is that of who serves the nation and who doesn't. The culture of protest is characterized by the passion of argument, whereas cultural dictatorship is only interested in the passion for violence.

In the Ramjas incident, even professors bore the brunt of violence. It was a vicious display of fascism out to muffle and scare the voices of dissent. As education in India has been split along ideological lines, the mores of ethical restraint have blurred. A Delhi University student, Gurmehar Kaur, protesting against the violence on her campus, drew national (and later international) attention for her social media protest. She posted a picture of herself holding a placard which said, 'I am a student of Delhi University. I am not afraid of ABVP. I am not alone. Every student of India is with me.' A BJP lawmaker retaliated by digging up a post Kaur had made the previous year about her father, an Indian soldier who died in the Kargil conflict in 1999. In response, Kaur held a placard which read, 'Pakistan did not kill my dad, war killed him.' Kaur's blaming the ideology of war, implicating both sides, was too disconcerting for the nationalists. Rape threats on the internet followed. A young woman taking the logic of war beyond territorial sentiments was too much for those who cannot imagine life beyond the enemy.

Nationalism, now reduced to hunting for enemies who think differently, is the enemy of thought. Fascist politics fears the sovereignty of thinking, and aims to subordinate it through violence. Fascism is pure, thoughtless violence, in search of a pure racial (and casteist) body. It is the violence of body over mind, the claims of a body trying to retain its purity against a mind that has been corrupted and contaminated by the *outsider*. Fascism seeks the most fortified territory of the self, where the *original* violence of a community is restored. The enemy alone gives life to fascism, which is consumed by its own obsession with death. It suffers, and makes others suffer, for an abstract idea of a lost community or nation that was *originally* perfect, illustrious and beautiful. Before the enemy entered their territory and spoiled it. In fascism, life and death are real questions, but the idea of suffering is abstract. This is where fascism differs crucially from religion, where the question of suffering is real and immediate. While the primary question for progressive political thought is not different from that of religion—i.e. how to address the problem of human suffering—it is also trapped by the idea of war against the (class) enemy.

The task of our era is perhaps to think beyond the idea of the enemy.

This is the promise of ethical thinking. Ethics is thinking

without the enemy, which by itself breaks the frontiers of territorial thought, and imagines a common ground of meeting and dwelling wherein, the enemy is the (potential) neighbour. Ethics is difficult politics, and it is the unique distinction of the Indian nationalist movement, that men like Gandhi, Ambedkar, and even Nehru, thought in nonviolent terms of resolving the political crisis with the British, as much as the problems within Indian society, through nonviolent methods. They were constantly able to think (and write) despite their various political engagements, only because they took the activity of thought seriously. In this sense, the Indian nationalist movement had a strong ethical streak. Thinking resists power nonviolently, for it hasn't given up on the promise of response.

The banal argument often made that Gandhi's nonviolent movement would have failed against Hitler, proves two things: one, that the Gandhian movement is relevant against all other forms of power, and two, that fascism is the most dangerous enemy of all ethical struggles against power. Fascism doesn't understand ethics, because it cannot exist without violence. In Ambedkar drinking water from the tank at Mahad in 1927, and Gandhi walking the lanes of Noakhali in 1946, barefoot, two powerful yet endearing images. In life as in politics, the most inspiring acts of courage are simultaneously a risk of one's vulnerability.

Postscript

On the Future of Politics

To advance without convictions and alone among the truths is not given to a man...
—E.M. Cioran, *A Short History of Decay*

The meteoric rise (and popular acceptance) of right-wing politics in significant parts of the world needs to make Left and liberal intellectuals who are critical defenders of democracy, rethink not only the predicaments of their time, but also their own political certainties. Something more has gone wrong than governmental policy, neoliberalism, and uninspiring leadership. To read the signs of our times, one needs to reflect more deeply on the rise of a certain regressive populism and political takeover by the Hindu Right in India. Despite the fundamental dissimilarities between Left politics and liberal political values and state policies, I would like to situate the crisis of both ideologies in a certain discourse of reason.

I shall also specifically argue against the idea of 'conviction'. The fire of conviction obscures, rather than illuminates, the limits of what is decisive in politics, or the politics of decisions, or, to use Carl Schmitt's term, 'decisionism'. Conviction does not allow us to see or understand what is wrong with decisionism, because it is part of the problem. It is necessary to probe into the roots of 'conviction' the way Nietzsche provokes us to, as much as to reconsider the more democratic idea of persuasion. A short trip through the contentions of Plato, Aristotle, Kant and Weber will give us an idea of what is at stake in this philosophical debate, for politics.

The distinction between conviction and persuasion has a bearing on politics, more precisely, on what constitutes decisions. A critique of political decisions and its relationship with violence is exemplified in Gandhi and Ambedkar, the two political thinkers who looked for a new politics of trust. For Gandhi, seeking trust works under the economy of persuasion. Ambedkar finds the social reluctance against trust embedded in the exclusionary social structures that other people. They provide directions to rethink the question of political ethics.

Writing under the growing shadow of fascism, one is overwhelmed by the competing ideologies of rationality. Modern political thought has been dominated by the discourse of Enlightenment reason. If fear of the state is responsible for the state of fear in (political) life, liberalism merely deflects that fear with juridical promises, and communism uses it to argue another state of fear and violence. There are many credible witness-narratives (in many genres) of the totalitarian fear unleashed by communist states. Albert Camus' argument against fear illuminates the necessity of persuasion in the political world.

The politics of rationality (and conviction) has privileged an inflexible idea of truth, neglecting the other side. Ambedkar and Gandhi, despite fundamental differences on the caste question and their approach towards modernity, favoured a nonviolent politics of trust. It is time to recover this much-neglected politics of trust. Trust is perhaps the best antidote against a politics of fear, currently being appropriated with disastrous consequences by the Hindu Right in India.

I

In the *Critique of Pure Reason*, Immanuel Kant makes a distinction between persuasion and conviction. For him, if the judgement of something being true is grounded in the 'character of a person', then it is termed persuasion. But if the judgement is held 'valid for every rational being, then its ground is objectively sufficient, and it is termed a conviction.' Kant distinguishes this idea of rational conviction from belief, saying 'Belief yields a conviction that is not communicable (because of its subjective ground).' The question of faith, or belief, lacks the ground for universal validity, as any moral law based on belief or faith can only remain binding upon the person propagating it. Its power of conviction and persuasion appears severely limited.

The idea of 'rational conviction' on which Kant based his universal ground of moral law has a contentious presence in the history and discourse of being. In history, the 'rational being' posing as universal agent of reason justified colonialism, and other structures of discrimination, exploitation and power. In discourse, the idea of universalism merged with scientific objectivity to proclaim an ungrounded philosophical premise (and standard) for all people to follow. The idea of (objective) thinking was divorced from the idea of (cultural) life. If universalism ignored real heterogeneity, there was a singular bias behind the idea of objectivity.

The idea of *relation* was ignored. Thinking, objectivity and knowledge, all occur *in relation to* communities. The idea of the individual and the Marxist idea of class as basic social categories for thought and knowledge, took on universal proportions. But their limits were posed by their relation to communities which shaped the individual and the politics of class. If we consider heterogeneity (and not universality) as the *real* ground for knowledge, thinking, and even the use of reason and conviction, then the claims of scientific validity get negated by something else. That something else is ethical thought, or the *thinking other*, which poses limits to Kantian thought.

II

Max Weber in his famous essay, 'Politics as a Vocation', contrasts two closely related concepts, the 'ethic of ultimate ends' or what is called the 'ethics of conviction' (*Gesinnungsethik*) with the 'ethics of responsibility' (*Verantwortungsethik*). If the 'ethics of conviction' is concerned with just political action irrespective of the outcome, the 'ethics of responsibility' is understood as consequentialist political action, where one feels accountable for one's actions. According to Weber, in the field of politics, these considerations are irreconcilable yet complimentary. Weber attempts to merge the influence of Christian morality in the 'ethics of conviction' with the process of secularization and rationalization (aided by the Calvinist tradition) in the 'ethics of responsibility'. But his hopeful search for an integrated ethic of action in modern politics remains fractured.

Weber's idea of *Gesinnungsethik* closely resembles Kant's belief-based conviction. Weber hinges an idea of ethics on belief-based conviction and shows how the advent of rationality slackens the role of conviction in political action (or decisions). He points to an internal rupture between conviction and ethics, once history passes from faith-based to reason-based political action. It raises a genealogical question regarding Kant's idea of 'rational conviction' and its relation to ethics.

III

The idea of conviction is fiercely challenged by Nietzsche's propositions. In section 55 of *The Antichrist*, Nietzsche attacks the idea of conviction. He first recollects his aphorism from *Human, All-Too-Human*: 'Convictions are more dangerous enemies of truth than lies.' Then he gives a genealogical account of conviction as an unreliable phenomenon: 'Every conviction has its history, its primitive forms, its stage of tentativeness and error: it becomes a conviction only after having been, for a long time, not one, and then, for an even longer time, hardly one. What if falsehood be also one of these embryonic forms of conviction?—Sometimes all that is needed is a change in persons: what was a lie in the father becomes a conviction in the son.' Nietzsche does not make the Kantian distinction between 'rational conviction' and the conviction that comes from faith or belief. The historical roots of reason, Nietzsche suggests, are not so rational. It makes the roots of (any form of) conviction, as suspect as beliefs tainted by lineage.

Nietzsche further explains: 'For example, the German historians are convinced that Rome was synonymous with despotism and that the Germanic peoples brought the spirit of liberty into the world: what is the difference between this conviction and a lie?' History, or rather, the belief in historical pride, and the tendency to demonize the other, Nietzsche suggests, needs conviction as much as conviction needs history. They feed into each other's false qualities. Conviction turns history on its head, surreptitiously making history speak the language of pride, be it the pride of race or ideology.

IV

In *Annihilation of Caste*, Ambedkar raises a striking question: 'Can you appeal to reason, and ask the Hindus to discard Caste as being contrary to reason? That raises the question: is a Hindu free to follow his reason?' Ambedkar is arguing for the value of reason and rues its lack or absence in the Hindu attached to the notion of caste. And yet, the second question introduces a prerequisite to the ability to use reason: *In order to use reason, you have to be free*. The Hindu is not free to use reason because he is tied to his notion of caste, his belief system. If people are not free to use reason, it means that reason isn't free from its context, and can be severely limited, if not altogether missing.

This contention questions the supposed universality of reason. But it does something more: *It poses freedom as a necessary condition for reason*. Is the modern world, which argues in favour of universal ideas (including freedom), free enough to claim universality? If not, how can its use of reason be free of its context, its social and cultural limitations and its (invisible) prejudices? Ambedkar's point echoes the Nietzchean perspective, by contending that the convictions of a Hindu disallow him to be free (to use reason). This contributes a perfectly crooked twist to Weber's point by suggesting that conviction manages to pass on its prejudices to reason.

V

Kant's critique of persuasion in the political realm is based on his dismissal of rhetoric. In *Critique of the Power of Judgement*, Kant writes: 'Rhetoric, insofar as by that is meant the art of persuasion, i.e. of deceiving by means of beautiful illusion (as an ars oratoria)...borrows from the art of poetry only as much as to win minds...and to rob them of their freedom:

thus it cannot be recommended either for the courtroom or for the pulpit.' For Kant, rhetoric is 'used for glossing over or concealing vice and error,' and amounts to nothing better than 'artful trickery'. It should have no place in law and religion, as both are meant to be discourses of truth. The lawyer and the priest are expected to tell the truth, not mislead people by using rhetorical devices. Modern demagogues use rhetoric to distract attention from their political misdeeds. But they can also use reason to justify their political agenda. The cunning of reason in politics works in insidious ways. For instance, nationalist passions can wear the garb of logical necessity. Territoriality limits the political imagination, where the logic of fear and threat are bordered by reason.

The roots of Kant's problem with rhetoric go back to Plato, who offers a negative verdict on rhetoric as well, equating it with flattery. In *Gorgias*, Socrates calls rhetoric 'a producer of persuasion,' and warns that it is 'not for instruction in the matter of right and wrong.' He likens rhetoric to a 'knack' (*empeiria* or experience), rather than an art or craft (*techne*). There is a bit more consideration accorded to rhetoric in *Phaedrus*, but this doesn't change Plato's position. Kant borrowed from Plato's discomfort, agreeing that rhetoric was a false and misleading art to convince audiences through passion rather than reason. The neat distinction in this argument gets messy when it comes to the politics of nationalism. People can be persuaded to accept violence through rationalist justifications. Fascist regimes have exploited this possibility. However, just as reason can persuade morally corrupt causes, the language of persuasion can also *politically* challenge nationalist rhetoric by appealing to ethics. Gandhi used ethical persuasion to quell communal violence in Noakhali. Trust is not based on reason, but on the reminders of the everyday, peaceful and ethical life of the community.

For Aristotle, however, persuasion plays a crucial part in the conception of rhetoric, which is a key element in politics. In *The Rhetoric*, Aristotle calls rhetoric 'the counterpart of dialectic'. But he holds that it contains three elements: reason, emotion and performativity. According to Aristotle, the character of the speaker contributes to the power of his persuasion. Rhetoric, in Aristotle's idea, is a complex art, whose truth-content cannot be judged by reason alone. Aristotle saw ethical possibility in persuasion. He argued that rhetoric is a challenging art of persuasion and the political actor must possess this quality if she wants to compete with others. He does not, however, equate the art of rhetoric with political wisdom but confines it to the contingency of necessity.

Plato and Kant's indictment of rhetoric as a deceptive, argumentative tool, failing to acknowledge its ethical content, is anti-political. Aristotle, in contrast, attributes credibility and genuineness to the relationship between rhetoric/persuasion and politics. Politics thrives on the ability to persuade people.

VI

In *Madness and Civilization*, Foucault avers that the 'language of psychiatry' is a 'monologue of reason *about* madness.' Foucault does a genealogical survey to show how reason is responsible for the way we understand its *other*, unreason and madness. He argued that reason in Greek philosophy, or Greek *logos*, 'had no contrary'. Reason in ancient Greece was dialogic, where it did not exclude its other. The discourse of reason was not exclusionist the way it turned out to be from the seventeenth century onwards. Critically responding to Foucault in his essay, 'Cogito and the History of Madness', Derrida invokes Søren Kierkegaard's statement: 'The instant of decision is madness.' There is an element of indeterminacy, of undecidability, at the moment of decision where reason falters. Decisions are central to politics, or, we can simply say, politics is about decisions.

As Carl Schmitt argued in *Political Theology*, the validity of a sovereign decision is based not upon the substance of the decision but on the *fact* that a decision has been taken. The sovereign proclaims the law by taking a decision. It includes for Schmitt, among other things, the *political* decision to name the enemy. Employing Kierkegaard's statement rhetorically, one may say that Schmitt's sovereign is only capable of taking mad decisions.

Ambedkar formulated the Buddhist idea of the 'need to kill', as a moment of reflection. One has to make a 'decision' regarding the necessity of violence. This juncture is the moment prior to the Schmittian moment of decision. It is a moment trembling with possibilities, where the decision to postpone or relinquish violence can take place. This is a moment of sovereign pause, where the question of violence is posed outside the will-to-violence. It is different from Gandhi's idea of passive resistance, which is a moral principle against any use of violence. Ambedkar's idea via Buddhism raises the question: *Is violence necessary?*

VII

Ambedkar's formulation of the 'need to kill' is a reminder of the legendary pause before the battle of Kurukshetra in *The Mahabharata*.

Reading Wilhelm von Humboldt's German translation of the *Gita*, Hegel, in his commentary on the text, is quite perplexed by the unique pause before war commences in Kurukshetra: 'Such a situation is of course contrary to all conceptions we Europeans have of war and of the moment when two great armies are confronting each other, ready to fight, and it is also contrary to...locate the meditation and presentation of an entire philosophical system in our study or elsewhere, yet certainly not in the mouth of the general and his charioteer at such a decisive hour.' At the 'decisive hour', *at the moment of decision*, when war has already been decided on by both parties, there is no European convention to stall it, and *rethink* the decision. It occasioned an unusually timed meditation on war, a meditation on the (nature of) the enemy itself, the enemy who is your own, one's other. It took place, in the first place, to assuage the warrior who, facing his opponent, hesitated to do battle.

The stunning nature of the image of Arjuna and Krishna on the chariot placed between the two armies about to go to war comes from the juxtaposition of two radically antithetical tendencies: war and introspection. Gandhi sees Arjuna's reluctance to fight, which is seemingly ethical, arising from a 'reason of delusion', where Arjuna makes a 'vain distinction' between kinsmen and others.

Arjuna does not satisfy Gandhi, because he does not raise the moral question about killing *as such*. For Gandhi, only posing the general, and by extension, universal question of violence is the moral necessity. Arjuna lacks commitment to the *principle* of nonviolence. Arjuna however *was* at war against his kinsmen. His question is contextually ethical. It is also a radical question for a Kshatriya to ask, for whom taking up arms is part of dharma. The faces of his kinsmen troubled Arjuna's conscience. It is only in the immediate sphere and moment of violence, facing the nearness of the other who is the enemy, that the ethical urgency of the question of violence is raised. Arjuna appeared to have lost the 'will to kill', facing his kinsmen, and paused on the question of necessity.

Gandhi's reading of the *Gita* manoeuvres to overcome the text's ethical limitations. He concedes that 'the Gita does not decide for us.' It did not decide for him for sure. For Gandhi, violence is impossible if one practises nonattachment to the ego. The lesson he draws from the image under discussion tries to dissolve the ethical conflict: 'We should identify ourselves with Arjuna and have faith that Shri Krishna is driving our chariot.'

VIII

It is the madness of politics, the madness of political decisions, which proclaims the enemy. If for Schmitt, politics is impossible without (naming) an enemy, for Gandhi, the political opponent is a potential friend. Delivering a speech at the YMCA auditorium in Madras, Gandhi said, 'For one who follows the doctrine of Ahimsa, there is no room for the enemy. Under this rule, there is no room for organised assassination, and there is no room for murders...'* Unlike the Schmittian understanding of politics as eternal enmity and just war, Gandhi's idea is based on expectations being the possibility of—and quest for—mutual justice. Gandhi's politics, instead of marking the animosity with another community as its territory, seeks to transform animosity to self-restraint and difficult friendship.

In the context of Hindu-Muslim relations, Gandhi wrote in *Young India* (29 May 1924), 'The Mussalmans are brave, they are generous and trusting the moment their suspicion is disarmed.' Then he points the finger at his own community: 'Hindus, living as they do in glass houses, have no right to throw stones at their Mussalman neighbours. See what we have done, are still doing, to the suppressed classes!' Gandhi equates the lack of generosity and trust with many fundamental ills: social suppression, hypocrisy, suspicion and fear. He is clear about whom the onus is on: 'The key to the situation lies with the Hindus. We must shed timidity or cowardice. We must be brave enough to trust and all will be well.' The enemy is born of fear. Distrust and fear breeds cowardice. In *Young India*

---

* *New India*, 16 February 1916.

(2 September 1926), Gandhi wrote, 'cowards can never be moral. Where there is fear there is no religion.' One of Ambedkar's subtitles in *Annihilation* underlines the social principle of life behind the lack of trust in Hindus: 'Caste deprives Hindus of mutual help, trust, and fellow-feeling.' The point is, for Hindus to develop a politics of trust, their internal hierarchy has to be dismantled.

The Noakhali massacre of 1948 tested Gandhi's politics. In an atmosphere of what Gandhi called 'terrible mutual distrust' in Noakhali, with a Muslim League administration accused of engineering the killing of Hindus, his confidence in nonviolence was shaken. Yet in his prayer meeting with a Hindu audience, Gandhi reiterated the need for trust, as it is 'beneath one's dignity to distrust a man's word without sufficient reason.' Despite the worst provocation, he held on to his ethical belief of 1925, 'Trust begets trust. Suspicion is fetid and only stinks.'

Gandhi's talks with Jinnah in 1944 on the subject of Partition constitute a historic document. It offers clues regarding Gandhi's willingness to cross boundaries set by conventional politics to negotiate peace and a sharing of power, in order to establish a genuine fraternity. For Gandhi, trust alone could work against the politics of suspicion. As early as in 1909, he wrote in *Hind Swaraj*: 'There is mutual distrust between the two communities. The Mahomedans, therefore, ask for certain concessions from Lord Morley. Why should the Hindus oppose this? If the Hindus desisted, the English would notice it, the Mahomedans would gradually begin to trust the Hindus, and brotherliness would be the outcome.' The failure of the Gandhi-Jinnah talks to avert the dark, looming possibility of Partition had monumental repercussions in Indian history. But it need not warrant any judgment on the failure of trust in politics.

IX

The Romanian cynic, E.M. Cioran, writes: 'Nothing monumental has emerged from dialogue, nothing explosive, nothing "great".' In his condemnation of dialogue, Cioran clarifies precisely what dialogue is *not* about. Dialogue does not aim for flamboyance or greatness. Dialogue is a means of listening to the other side, which is the only way to foster humility. The dialogical approach demonstrates that convictions do not hold the last word in politics. The truth of the matter lies between two convictions, where earnestness matters, not victory. Conviction does not contribute to truth, for it looks to win (the argument). If politics is understood as a confrontation of interests and ideas, it is neither served by fascist or communist victory, nor by liberal compromise.

X

The problem of the political decision and its relation to violence, however, persists and haunts modern politics and political thought. The problem of the political decision is intrinsically related to the problem of modern time. The sense of urgency and corresponding restlessness to seize time, to mark a date for victory (or defeat) in advance, marks most political movements, including the project of the revolutionary seizure of power. Decisions are timed, and considered timely, and therein lies the connection between decisionism and time. Buber offers two key reservations regarding this problem, in his critique of politics in modern time.

Buber raises the problem of calculability. In September 1920, Gandhi wrote a piece where he spoke of the possibility of attaining Swaraj 'in a year', if Indians followed the principles of satyagraha. Buber's response was: 'One may be certain of the truthfulness and non-violence...but not of the attainment of Swaraj in one year. "In one year" is a political word; the religious watchword must read: Some time, perhaps today, perhaps in a century. In religious reality there is no stipulation of time.' Waiting for justice, for establishing truth, cannot fall under the language of calculability. To calculate time is to measure the costs of success and failure, to constrict an ethical gesture or demand by temporal consideration and anxiety.

Benjamin's idea of messianic time (and politics) in his famous *Theses on the Philosophy of History*, is a double helix, part theology and part materialism, part Judeo-Christian and part Marxist. Benjamin imagines a 'messianic zero-hour', where the many pasts of oppression are redeemed. Revolutionary memory endangers the continuity of time and the cosy relationship between past and present. Time does not free us from history, labour does. But labour is trapped within the structure of time, exploitatively ruled by the wealthy. To free labour and its unhinged possibilities, a singular moment in historical time has to be realized. What messianic time disrupts and shocks is a series of commodified relations between people and things. It is a liberating idea that is made possible by bringing together the principles of redemption and revolution.

Buber's perspective is different. In his dialogue with Gandhi, he writes: 'We cannot prepare the messianic world, we can only prepare *for it*. There is no legitimately messianic, no legitimately messianically-intended politics' (Emphasis added). The question of messianism as a redemptive idea is original to Judaic thought. The messianic moment, Buber thinks, cannot be blueprinted upon history. The world can only prepare the grounds for such a moment to arrive, where the conflicts of history find respite. Is it possible to bring redemption through revolutionary action? The idea of redemption is a spiritual idea which Benjamin seeks by purely materialist means and thinking. How does Benjamin reconcile the purely materialist idea of 'resurrected humanity', by employing 'the services of theology'? Do the services of theology come without a price? Benjamin mentions 'victory' and the necessity to 'win' in *Thesis I.*

For Buber, Paul Mendes-Flohr finely sums up the political desire spurring revolutionary action, which seeks to 'expedite redemption', to 'hasten the advent of a world redeemed of injustice and human suffering', as misguided and revelatory of the crisis of messianic politics. Buber regards the frayed relation between time and history, not as something to be overcome, but as something to be healed. The modern political desire to overcome history is fraught with a baseless presupposition that history, in the first place, can be *overcome*. Can such an overcoming be guaranteed by mere conviction? What if a revolutionary moment, does not, cannot *overcome*? What price does the world pay for its failure?

XI

In Europe's turbulent 1940s, Camus wrote a series of articles for *Combat* magazine. In his very first piece, 'The Century of Fear', Camus mourns the end of a 'long dialogue' between human beings. He notes that 'a man who *cannot be persuaded* is a man who makes others afraid' (Emphasis added). Two characteristic figures of twentieth-century Europe immediately come to mind: the Fascist and the Sartrean, the right-wing and the left-wing ideologue, who cannot accept the truth *otherwise*. They aren't open to ideas outside their own beliefs and hide facts that contradict those beliefs. They contributed, as Camus puts it, to the 'vast conspiracy of silence'. Camus saw it as the condition of terror, and explains it brilliantly: 'We live in terror because persuasion is no longer possible, because man has been delivered entirely into the hands of history and can no longer turn toward that part of himself which is as true as the historic part, and which he discovers when he discovers the beauty of the world and of people's faces.' Camus' acute observations in the dark times of European politics corroborates the Aristotelian point about persuasion. Fear and terror pose limits to (political) life. The politics of conviction, aided by reason, repeatedly strikes its head (and ours) against the imaginary wall of belief systems. The old pleasure of listening to others has to be reintroduced in politics, not as a formal scheme, but as an opening up of thinking beyond certainties.

In his book, *Danube*, Italian writer Claudio Magris briefly mentions his philosopher-compatriot and writer, Carlo Michelstaedter, who had killed himself at a very young age. Magris writes that, for Michelstaedter (in his famous work *Persuasion and Rhetoric*), 'conviction or persuasion was *peitho*, a Greek word, and Greek words have the dual number.' It is curious that both persuasion and conviction have a common etymology in Greek, even as they branched out into opposing ideas in philosophy. The initial meaning of *peitho* in Greek, which was further explored in Hebrew, is closer to 'trust' than conviction. Modern politics based on convictions has lost our trust. Conviction is rooted in identity. Identity is the incurable limit, where the other cannot be born. Trust needs the dismantling of old structures and their hesitations, to find its way back into our hearts. Trust is the future of politics.

Acknowledgements

Gratitude is due to *The Wire*, where I have most frequently contributed in the last couple of years. Siddharth Varadarajan's editorial attention has been an immensely motivating experience. To *The New York Times*, for publishing my article defending free speech and ideas. Thanks to Basharat Peer for fine editorial and writerly advice. To *The Economic and Political Weekly*, for publishing two short essays on Nehru and the crisis of nationalism. To *Outlook*, for publishing my piece on Aurobindo. To *The Hindu*, for publishing my tribute to the iconic Dalit scholar, Rohith Vemula.

I am indebted to Jitendra Kumar for introducing my work to Ravi Singh. Ravi's interest and persuasive suggestions, not only as an editor but as a reader, transformed the initial project into something more ambitious and intellectually stimulating.

I am grateful to Ramesh Mallipeddi for introducing me to Emmanuel Levinas. To Udaya Kumar, for generously sharing his insights on Gandhi. To Sudipta Kaviraj, for sharing his views on Nehru during my dissertation from his abandoned essay, 'The Man Who Discovered India'. To Ajay Skaria, for sending his essay on Gandhi, and his fine arguments on Gandhi's ethics. To Rajeev Bhargava, my supervisor at JNU, for his lectures on Hegel, his course on nationalism, and for bringing Charles Taylor to the classroom one wintry morning to speak about the 'social imaginary'. To three memorable intellectual moments at JNU: Michael Taussig, presenting a draft from his book, *The Magic of the State*, Jacques Derrida, speaking on his Algerian childhood, and Howard Caygill's new findings on Walter Benjamin and Kafka.

To Gopal Guru for his warm encouragements, and generous remarks on my work. To Talal Asad, for agreeing to read this manuscript amidst an anguished period of his life, and making an unreturnable gesture. To Susie Tharu, for reading and endorsing my manuscript in the middle of her travels and commitments. To Aishwary Kumar, for long-distance conversations on Ambedkar, and helping to formulate a couple of arguments in the book. To Avantika, for feminist references, and her bright company. To Richa, for helping with sections of the manuscript, and everything else. To Kartikeya, for a keen editorial eye, and invaluable comments that perfected the book beyond expectations.

To my mother, who took care of her children first, gods later. To no kith and kin. To friends not intimidated by morality (morality, like love, is incurable), in trust and solidarity, over days and nights of stirring the pan, pouring the wine and playing music, over provocative disagreements, lively quarrels and unspoken fondness.

Bibliography

Ambedkar, B.R. 'The Annihilation of Caste,' In *Dr. Babasaheb Ambedkar: Writings and Speeches Volume 1*. Bombay: Education Department, Government of Maharashtra, 1979.

——— 'The Buddha and his Dhamma,' In *Dr. Babasaheb Ambedkar: Writings and Speeches Volume 11*. Bombay: Education Department, Government of Maharashtra, 1992.

——— 'Buddha or Karl Marx,' In *Dr. Babasaheb Ambedkar: Writings and Speeches Volume 3*. Bombay: Education Department, Government of Maharashtra, 1987.

——— 'Castes in India: Their Mechanism, Genesis and Development', In *Dr. Babasaheb Ambedkar: Writings and Speeches, Volume 1*. Bombay: Education Department, Government of Maharashtra, 1979, p. 3-22.

——— 'Gandhi and His Fast,' In *Dr. Babasaheb Ambedkar: Writings and Speeches Volume 5*. Bombay: Education Department, Government of Maharashtra, 1989.

——— 'Pakistan or the Partition of India,' In *Dr. Babasaheb Ambedkar Writings and Speeches Volume 8*, Bombay: Education Department , Government of Maharashtra, 1990.

——— 'Philosophy of Hinduism,' In *Dr. Babasaheb Ambedkar: Writings and Speeches Volume 3*. Bombay: Education Department, Government of Maharashtra, 1987.

——— 'Revolution and Counter-Revolution in Ancient India,' In *Dr. Babasaheb Ambedkar: Writings and Speeches Volume 3*. Bombay: Education Department, Government of Maharashtra, 1987.

―――― *What Congress and Gandhi have done to the Untouchables*. Bombay: Thacker, 1946.

―――― 'Untouchables or The Children of India's Ghetto,' In *Dr. Babasaheb Ambedkar: Writings and Speeches Volume 5*, Bombay: Education Department, Government of Maharashtra, 1989.

―――― *The Untouchables: Who Were They and Why They Became Untouchables?* Delhi: Amrit Book Company, 1948.

Anderson, Benedict. *Imagined Communities* (extended edition). London: Verso, 1991.

Appadurai, Arjun. *Fear of Small Numbers: An Essay on the Geography of Anger*. Durham: Duke University Press, 2006.

Aristotle. *De Anima (On the Soul)*. Translated by Hugh Lawson-Tancred. London: Penguin Books, 1986.

―――― *The Poetics of Aristotle: Translation and Commentary*, Edited by Stephen Halliwell. North Carolina: The University of North Carolina Press, 1987.

―――― *Aristotle's Politics*. Translated by Carnes Lord. Chicago: University of Chicago Press, 1984.

Asad, Talal. *Formations of the Secular: Christianity, Islam, Modernity*. Stanford: Stanford University Press, 2003.

Aurobindo, Sri. 'Bal Gangadhar Tilak', In *Early Cultural Writings (1890-1910)*. https://www.aurobindo.ru/workings/sa/37_01/0145_e.htm

―――― *The Life Divine, The Complete Works of Sri Aurobindo* (Volume 21 & 22). Pondicherry: Sri Aurobindo Ashram Trust, 2005.

―――― 'The Office and Limitations of the Reason,' In *The Complete Works of Sri Aurobindo* (Volume 25). Pondicherry: Sri Aurobindo Ashram Trust, 1997.

―――― 'On a Proposed Visit by Jawaharlal Nehru,' In

Autobiographical Notes And Other Writings of Historical Interest. https://www.aurobindo.ru/workings/sa/37_36/0345_e.htm.

———'The Secret of the Veda,' In *The Complete Works of Sri Aurobindo* (Volume 15). Pondicherry: Sri Aurobindo Ashram Trust, 1998.

———*Sri Aurobindo: Nationalism, Religion, and Beyond—Writings on Politics, Society, and Culture*. Edited by Peter Heehs. New Delhi: Permanent Black, 2005.

Bauman, Zygmunt. 'Parvenu and Pariah: heroes and victims of modernity,' In *The Politics of Postmodernity*, Edited by Irving Velody. Cambridge: Cambridge University Press, 1998.

———*Strangers at our Door*. Cambridge, USA: Polity Press, 2016.

Benjamin, Walter. *Illuminations*. Translated by Harry Zohn. New York: Harcourt Brace Jovanovich, Inc., 1968.

———*Reflections: Essays, Aphorisms, Autobiographical Writings*. Translated by Edmund Jephcott and Edited by Peter Demetz. New York: Harcourt Brace Jovanovich, Inc., 1978.

Berlin, Isaiah. 'Two Concepts of Liberty,' In *The Proper Study of Mankind*, Edited Henry Hardy and Roger Hausheer. London: Pimlico Edition, 1998.

Bhabha, Homi. *Narrating the Nation*. London: Routledge, 1990.

Bhattacharjee, Manash Firaq. 'The Cryptic Suicide of a Dalit Scholar.' *The Wire* (18 March, 2017). https://thewire.in/caste/cryptic-suicide-another-dalit-scholar-rajni-krish

Bilgrami, Akeel. 'Two Concepts of Secularism,' In *Politics in India*, Edited by Sudipta Kaviraj. New Delhi: Oxford University Press, 1997.

Bose, Nirmal Kumar. *My Days with Gandhi*. Delhi: Orient Longman Limited, 1974.

Buber, Martin. *Pointing the Way: Collected Essays*. Translated by Maurice Freidman. New York: Harper & Brothers, 1957.

Bühler, Georg. *The Laws of Manu*. Oxford: Clarendon Press, 1886.

Butalia, Urvashi. *The Other Side of Silence: Voices from the Partition of India*. New Delhi: Penguin Books, 1998.

Camus, Albert. *Camus at 'Combat': Writing 1944-1947*, Translated by Arthur Goldhammer, Edited by Jacqueline Lévi-Valensi. New Jersey: Princeton University Press, 2006.

Chatterjee, Partha. 'In Kashmir, India Is Witnessing Its General Dyer Moment.' *The Wire* (June 2, 2017). https://thewire.in/government/general-dyer-indian-army-kashmir.

——— *Nationalist Thought and the Colonial World: A Derivative Discourse?* New Delhi: Oxford University Press, 1986.

Chaudhuri, Nirad. C. *Thy Hand, Great Anarch! India 1921-1952*. London: The Hogarth Press, 1987.

Choudhury, Soumyabrata. *Ambedkar and Other Immortals: An Untouchable Research Programme*. New Delhi: Navayana, 2018.

Chomsky, Noam. 'On Social Media, India's Aadhaar System, China, #Metoo and the Left Today: Noam Chomsky Interviewed by Swagat Baruah,' *The Forum: Journal of Political Theory and Philosophy*, March 14, 2018. http://jptp.online/wp-content/uploads/2018/03/Noam-CHomsky-Final.pdf.

Cioran, E.M. *A Short History of Decay*. Translated by Richard Howard. London: Quartet, 1990.

Derrida, Jacques, *Adieu to Emmanuel Levinas*. Translated by Pascale-Anne Brault and Michael Naas. Stanford: Stanford University Press, 1999.

―――― *The Other Heading: Reflections on Today's Europe*. Translated by Pascale-Anne Brault and Michael Naas. Bloomington: Indiana University Press, 1992.

―――― *The Politics of Friendship*. Translated by George Collins. London: Verso, 2005.

―――― *Specters of Marx: The State of the Debt, the Work of Mourning, and the New International*. Translated by Peggy Kamuf. London: Psychology Press, 1994.

―――― *Writing and Difference*. Translated by Alan Bass. Chicago: University of Chicago Press, 1978.

Dixit, Neha. 'Shadow Lines,' *Outlook* (4 August, 2014). https://www.outlookindia.com/magazine/story/shadow-lines/291494.

Engineer, Asghar Ali. *Muslim Minority: Continuity and Change*. New Delhi: Gyan Publishing House, 2009.

Fanon, Frantz. *The Wretched of the Earth*. Translated by Constance Farrington. New York: Grove Weidenfeld, 1963.

Farah, Nuruddin. 'Childhood of my schizophrenia,' *Times Literary Supplement*, November 23-29, 1990.

Foucault, Michel. *The Birth of Biopolitics: Lectures at the Collège de France 1978-1979*. Translated by Graham Burchell. New York: Picador, 2008.

―――― *Discipline & Punish: The Birth of the Prison*. Translated by Alan Sheridan. New York: Vintage Books, 1995.

―――― *Ethics: Subjectivity and Truth*, Edited by Paul Rabinow. Translated by Robert Hurley and others. New York: The New Press, 1994. https://monoskop.org/images/0/00/Foucault_Michel_Ethics_Subjectivity_and_Truth.pdf

―――― *The Politics of Truth*, Edited by Sylvere Lotringer. Translated by Lysa Hochroth and Catherine Porter. Los Angeles: Semiotext(e), 1997.

———— *Madness and Civilisation: A History of Insanity in the Age of Reason*. Translated by Richard Howard. Oxon: Routledge Classics, 1989.

Gandhi, M.K. *An Autobiography or the Story of My Experiments with Truth* (Critical Edition), Edited by Tridip Suhrud. Translated by Mahadev Desai. Gurgaon: Penguin Books, 2018.

———— *The Bhagavad Gita According to Gandhi*, Edited by John Strohmeier. Berkeley, USA: North Atlantic Books, 2009.

———— *The Collected Works of Mahatma Gandhi*, Volume LVIII. New Delhi: The Publication Division, 1974.

———— *The Collected Works of Mahatma Gandhi*, Volume LIX. New Delhi: The Publication Division, 1974.

———— *The Collected Works of Mahatma Gandhi*, Volume LXXXVI. New Delhi: The Publication Division, 1982.

———— *Hind Swaraj*, Edited by Parel, Anthony. Cambridge: Cambridge University Press, 1990.

———— *The Gandhi Reader*, Edited by Rudrangshu Mukherjee. New Delhi: Penguin Books, 1993.

Gandhi, Manubahen. *The Lonely Pilgrim: Gandhiji's Noakhali Pilgrimage*. Ahmedabad: Navjivan Publishing House, 1964.

Godse, Nathuram Vinayak and Gopal Vinayak Godse. *Why I Assassinated Gandhi*. Delhi: Surya Bharti Prakashan, 1993.

Grass, Gunter. *The Flounder*. Translated by Ralph Manheim. London: Picador, 1989.

Guru, Gopal. *Humiliation: Claims and Contexts*. New Delhi: Oxford University Press, 2009.

———— 'A Tragic Exit from Social Death' *Outlook*, February 1, 2016. https://www.outlookindia.com/magazine/story/a-tragic-exit-from-social-death/296480.

———'Taking Nationalism Seriously,' In *What the Nation Really Needs to Know: The JNU Nationalism Lectures*, Edited by Rohit Azad, Janaki Nair, Mohinder Singh and Mallarika Sinha Roy. Delhi: HarperCollins, 2017.

Haavikko, Paavo. 'The Power Game,' Translated by David Barrett, In *Books from Finland: A Literary Journal* 2, 1984.

Hall, Stuart, 'The West and the Rest,' In *Modernity: An Introduction to Modern Societies*. Oxon: Routledge, 1996.

Hegel, Georg Wilhelm Friedrich. *Philosophy of Right*. Translated by S.W. Dyde. New York: Cosmo Classics, 2008.

———*Reason in History: A General Introduction to the Philosophy of History*. Translated by Robert S. Hartman. Indianapolis: The Bobbs-Merrill Company, 1953.

———*On the Episode of the Mahabharata Known by the Name Bhagavad-Gita by Wilhelm Von Humboldt*, Edited and Translated by Herbert Herring. New Delhi: Indian Council of Philosophical Research, 1995.

Heidegger, Martin. *Poetry, Language, Thought*. Translated by Albert Hofstadter. New York: Harper Perennial, 2001.

Jafri, Ali Sardar. 'Ali Sardar Jafri: The Youthful Boatman of Joy,' Edited by Squadron Leader Anil Sehgal. New Delhi: Bharatiya Jnanpith, 2001.

Kant, Immanuel. *Critique of Pure Reason*. Translated by Paul Guyer. New York: Cambridge University Press, 1998.

———*Critique of the Power of Judgement*. Translated by Paul Guyer. New York: Cambridge University Press, 2001.

Kar, Bodhisattva. '"Tongue Has No Bone": Fixing the Assamese Language, c. 1800–c. 1930.' *Studies in History* (February 1, 2008), 27-76

Kojève, Alexandre. *Introduction to the Reading of Hegel: Lectures on the Phenomenology of Spirit.* Translated by James H. Nichols Jr. Ithaca: Cornell University Press, 1980.

Kumar, Aishwary. 'The Ellipsis of Touch: Gandhi's Unequals.' *Public Culture* 23, No. 2 (Spring 2011), 449-469.

——— *Radical Equality: Ambedkar, Gandhi and the Risk of Democracy.* Stanford: Stanford University Press, 2015.

Lenin, V.I. '"What Is to Be Done?" and Other Writings,' In *Essential Works of Lenin*, Edited by Henry M. Christman. New York: Dover Publications Inc., 1987.

Levinas, Emmanuel. *Emmanuel Levinas: Basic Philosophical Writings*, Edited by Adriaan T. Peperzak, Simon Critchley and Robert Bernasconi. Bloomington: Indiana University Press, 1996.

——— *The Levinas Reader*, Edited by Seán Hand. Oxford: Basil Blackwell, 1989.

——— *Otherwise than Being or Beyond Essence.* Translated by Alphonso Lingis. Dordrecht, Netherlands: Kluwer Academic Publishers, 1991.

Lindsay, James. 'The Philosophy of Schelling.' *The Philosophical Review* 19, No. 3 (May, 1910), 259-275.

Magris, Claudio. *Danube.* Translated by Patrick Creagh. New York: Farrar Strauss Giroux, 1989.

Mamdani, Mahmood. *Good Muslim, Bad Muslim: America, the Cold War, and the Roots of Terror.* New Delhi: Permanent Black, 2004.

Manto, Sadat Hasan. *Mottled Dawn: Fifty Sketches and Stories of Partition.* Translated by Khalid Hasan. New Delhi: Penguin India, 2012.

——— *Stars from Another Sky: The Bombay Film World in the 1940s.* Translated by Khalid Hasan. New Delhi: Penguin India, 2014.

Marx, Karl. *The German Ideology*, (trans.) C.J. Arthur, International Publishers, New York, 2007.

———*Theories of Surplus Value*, (trans.) G.A Bonner and Emile Burns, Lawrence and Wishart, London, 1951.

———'On the Jewish Question,' In *The Marx–Engels Reader*. Translated by Robert Tucker. New York: Norton & Company, 1978.

Mehta, Bhanu Pratap. 'Sinking Valley.' *The Indian Express* (April 15, 2017). https://indianexpress.com/article/opinion/columns/sinking-valley-kashmir-violence-stone-pelting-pm-modi-upa-4613509/.

Mendes-Flohr, Paul. 'The Kingdom of God. Martin Buber's Critique of Messianic Politics.' *Behemoth: A Journal on Civilisation* 2 (2008), 26–38.

Menon, Dilip M. 'Being a Marxist the Brahmin Way: E.M.S Nambudiripad and the Pasts of Kerala,' In *Invoking the Past: The Uses of History*, Edited by Daud Ali. Oxford: Oxford University Press, 1999.

Nag, Sajal. 'Nehru and the Nagas: Minority Nationalism and the Post-Colonial State,' *Economic and Political Weekly* 44, No. 49 (December 5-11, 2009), 48-55.

Nandy, Ashis. *The Intimate Enemy*. New Delhi: Oxford University Press, 1983.

———'Obituary of a Culture,' *Seminar* 513 (May 2002), 15-18.

Nehru, Jawaharlal. *An Autobiography*. New Delhi: Oxford University Press, 1980.

———*The Discovery of India*, Oxford University Press, Jawaharlal Nehru Memorial Fund, 1964.

———*The Essential Writings*, Vol. 1, Edited by S. Gopal. New Delhi: Oxford University Press, 2003.

———*Glimpses of World History*. New Delhi: Jawaharlal Nehru Memorial Fund, 1982.

―――― *India Today and Tomorrow, Azad Memorial Lectures*. New Delhi: Indian Council for Cultural Relations, 1960.

Nietzsche, Friedrich. *The Anti-Christ*. Translated by H.L. Mencken. New York: Alfred A. Knopf, 1918.

―――― *Beyond Good and Evil: Prelude to a Philosophy of the Future*. Translated by R.J. Hollingdale. London: Penguin Books, 1973.

Norman, Dorothy. *Nehru: The First Sixty Years, Volume 2*. Bombay: Asia Publishing House, 1965.

Omvedt, Gail. *Dalits and the Democratic Revolution: Dr. Ambedkar and the Dalit Movement in Colonial India*. New Delhi: Sage Publications India, 2014.

Paz, Octavio. 'Nehru: Man of Two Cultures & One World.' New Delhi: Indian National Commission for Cooperation with UNESCO, 1967.

―――― *One Earth, Four or Five Worlds: Reflections on Contemporary History*. Translated by Helen R. Lane. New York: Harcourt Brace Jovanovich, Inc., 1986.

―――― *The Labyrinth of Solitude*. Translated by Lysander Kemp. London: Allen Lane/Penguin, 2005.

Pessoa, Fernando. *The Book of Disquiet*, Edited and Translated by Richard Zenith. London: Penguin Books, 1998.

Rushdie, Salman. *Imaginary Homelands: Essays and Criticism 1981–1991*. London: Random House, 2010.

―――― *Shame*. New York: Random House, 1983.

Samaddar, Ranabir. *The Nation Form: Essays on Indian Nationalism*. New Delhi: Sage Publications, 2012.

Saramago, José. *Blindness*. Translated by Giovanni Pontiero. London: Harvill Press, 1997.

Sarasvati, Pandita Ramabai. *The High-caste Hindu Woman*. Pune: Maharashtra State Board for Literature and Culture, 1981.

Sarukkai, Sundar. 'Phenomenology of Untouchability,' *Economic and Political Weekly* 44, No. 37 (2009), 39-48.

Schmitt, Carl. *The Concept of the Political*. Translated by George Schwab. Chicago: University of Chicago Press, 2007.

——— *Political Theology: Four Chapters on the Concept of Sovereignty*. Translated by George Schwab. Chicago: University of Chicago Press, 1985.

Sengupta, Debjani. 'A City Feeding on Itself: Testimonies and Histories of 'Direct Action Day,' In *Sarai Reader: Turbulence* 6 (2006), 288-295.

Seth, Sanjay. 'Nehruvian Socialism – 1927-37: Nationalism, Marxism, and the Pursuit of Modernity,' *Alternatives* 18, No. 4 (1993), 453-473.

Singh, Mohinder. 'Tagore on Modernity, Nationalism and "the Surplus in Man,"' *Economic and Political Weekly* 52, No. 19 (2017), 46-52.

Skaria, Ajay. 'The Strange Violence of Satyagraha: Gandhi, Itihaas, and History,' In *Heterotopias: Nationalism and the Possibility of History in South Asia*, Edited by Manu Bhagwan. New Delhi: Oxford University Press, 2010.

Sukirtharani. 'Interview: A Dalit Poet's Explorations Into Discrimination and the Female Body.' *The Wire* (16 July, 2017). https://thewire.in/caste/dalit-poet-discrimination-female-body-poetry.

Tagore, Rabindranath. 'Civilization and Progress,' In *Rabindranath Tagore: Selected Essays*. New Delhi: Rupa & Company, 2004.

——— *Nationalism*. New Delhi: Penguin Books, 2009.

——— *The Religion of Man*. New Delhi: Rupa & Company, 2005.

Tagore, Rabindranath, and M.K. Gandhi. *The Mahatma and The Poet: Letters and Debates between Gandhi and Tagore 1915-1941*, Compiled and Edited by Sabyasachi Bhattacharya. New Delhi: National Book Trust, 1997.

Tambe, Ashwini. 'Gandhi's "Fallen" Sisters: Difference and the National Body Politic,' *Social Scientist* 37, No. 1/2 (Jan–Feb, 2009), 21-38.

Taylor, Charles. *The Sources of the Self: The Making of Modern Identity*. Cambridge: Cambridge University Press, 1989.

Triadafilopoulos, Triadafilos. 'Politics, Speech, and the Art of Persuasion: Toward an Aristotelian Conception of the Public Sphere.' *The Journal of Politics* 61, No. 3 (1999), 741-757.

Verstraeten, Johan. 'The Tension Between "Gesinnungsethik" and "Verantwortungsethik": A Critical Interpretation of the Position of Max Weber in "Politik als Beruf",' *Ethical Perspectives* 2, No. 3 (1995), 180-187.

Virilio, Paul. *Popular Defense of Ecological Struggles*. Translated by Mark Polizzotti. New York: Semiotext(e), 1990.

Vivekananda, Swami. *The Complete Works of Swami Vivekananda* Volume III. Mayavati, Almora: Advaita Ashrama, 1964.

——— *The Complete Works of Swami Vivekananda* Volume VI. Mayavati, Almora: Advaita Ashrama, 1964.

Waikar, Namita. 'When Shalubai won the chair, but lost the table,' *People's Archive of Rural India* (29 November, 2016). https://ruralindiaonline.org/articles/when-shalubai-won-the-chair-but-lost-the-table.

Walzer, Michael. 'Nation and Universe,' In The Tanner Lectures On Human Values, Brasenose College, Oxford University, May 1989.

Index

Aadhaar Act, 128
Aadhaar card, debate on, 123–129
Aadhaar-enabled Public Distribution System (AePDS), 124
active resistance, 16
Afrazul, Mohammad, 137
Ahmed, Najeeb, 147–149
Akhil Bharatiya Vidyarthi Parishad (ABVP), 161–162
Ambedkar, 80
   annihilation of caste, 110, 118–122, 160–161, 172
   caste and Hindu society, 49–51
   coming of Buddhism, 55–56, 60, 121, 175
   debate with Gandhi, 153–161
   distinction between 'will' and 'need', 160
   formulation of need to kill, 159–160, 175
   Hindu consciousness, 51
   idea of conversion, 120–122
   Marxist idea of labour and caste, 59
   modern form of untouchability, 55–58
   nationalism, 51–52
   relationship between Hindus and untouchables, 52
   social justice, 67
   universal principle, 119
   The Untouchables: Who Were They? And Why They Became Untouchables, 55
   Untouchables or The Children of India's Ghetto, 52
   widow and widower in Hindu society, 54
Ananthamurthy, U.R., 85
Anderson, Benedict, 1, 51
Antya, 56–58
Aristotle, 106, 174
Armed Forces Special Powers Act of 1958 (AFSPA), 14, 131
army-civilian conflict, Kashmir, 129–133
Asad, Talal
   Formations of the Secular: Christianity, Islam, Modernity, 82
   secular State, 82–83
Assam Accord, 1985, 77
Assam Disturbed Areas Act, 1955, 14
Assam Movement, 68, 74–76
   communal nature of, 76
Aurobindo, Sri, 16
   future of divine law, 19–20
   Hindu-Muslim relations, 20–22
   Hindu nationalism, 22–23
   idea and act of sacrifice, 19
   idea of a nation-state as divine manifestation, 23
   modernity and development of modern state, 18
   nationalism, 20
   nation-as-mother, idea of, 17, 21
   notions of 'sacred' and 'divine', 18–19
   political patriotism, 21
   'real problem' of Muslim rule in India, 21
   Vedas, 19
Ayaz, Farid, 95–96
A.Z. Phizo-led Naga insurgency, 14
Azad, Maulana Abdul Kalam, 98

Bhabha, Homi
   Narrating the Nation, 11
   nationalist reconstruction, 11–12
Babri Masjid incident, 83, 86, 137
Bauman, Zygmunt, 11
   immigrants/refugees, 73

Bengal's Partition of 1947, 87–88
Benjamin, Walter, 19, 113, 180
  One Way Street, 72
  Theses on the Philosophy of History, 69
Berlin, Isaiah, 34
Bhandarkar, D. R., 55
Bhat, Qaisar Ahmad, 133
Bhushan, Ashok, 124
Bilgrami, Akeel, 82
Bombay riots, 87
Bose, Nirmal Kumar, 45–46, 48–49
Brahminical body, 107–108
Brahminical caste system, 159
Brecht, Bertolt, 73, 113, 116
Buber, Martin, 179–181
Buddhism, 55, 71
Butalia, Urvashi, 99

Camus, Albert, 168, 181–182
Cape of Good Hope, 2
caste system. *see also* untouchables/untouchability
  Ambedkar's view, 49–51, 105–106, 108, 110, 118–122, 160–161
  Hegel's views, 53
  Namboodiripad's view, 59
  Nehru's view, 4
Celan, Paul, 113
Chatterjee, Partha, 5, 10, 42–43, 131
Chaudhuri, Nirad C., 87
Chomsky, Noam, 128
Choudhury, Soumyabrata, 120, 163
Cioran, E.M., 179
classical utilitarianism, 31
Columbus, Christopher, 2
conviction, idea of, 167–169, 182
  belief-based, 179
  ethics of, 179
  rational, 169–170

Dabholkar, Narendra, 84
da Gama, Vasco, 2
Dalits, 58, 66, 113
Dar, Farooq Ahmad, 130–133

Dasgupta, Satish Chandra, 45
dates, 62–63
democracy, 63, 74
democratic collectivism, 5
democratic values, 15
Derrida, Jacques, 52, 57, 60, 63, 86, 107
  poetic faith, 94
  The Politics of Friendship, 90
Divan, Shyam, 128–129
Dixit, Neha, 145

Engineer, Asghar Ali, 83
Evans, Brad, 78

Fanon, Frantz, 156–161
  relationship between truth and nationalism, 157
  The Wretched of the Earth, 157
fascism, 165, 168
Filliozat, Jean, 41
Foucault, Michel, 124, 127
  Madness and Civilization, 174
fraternity, 64–65
freedom, 65–67

Gandhi, 1, 173, 179–180
  The Annihilation of Caste, 80
  association with spinning wheel, 40–41
  being Hindu, 80, 84
  brahmacharya, idea of, 48–49
  conception of inequality, 109
  Dandi March, 1930, 152
  debate with Ambedkar, 153–161
  debate with Tagore, 24, 32, 38–40
  dharma/tradition, 17
  distinction between the West and India, 37–38
  friendship, 64
  Hindu-Muslim relations, 44–49, 177–178
  history, idea of, 42
  national movement against British rule, 43–44
  nonviolence, idea of, 41–42, 44, 60, 152–153, 160, 166

politics of truth, 64
project of swaraj, 16, 37
question of justice between Hindus and Muslims, 88–90
reading of the *Gita*, 175–177
satyagraha, 16, 39, 41–42, 44, 46, 49, 64, 111–112, 153
truth, 157–159
German Romanticism, 27
Godse, Nathuram, 84–85, 155
Gogoi, Major Leetul, 131
Government of India Act 1935, 14
Gramsci, Antonio, 151
Gujarat anti-Muslim pogrom, 2002, 87, 100
Guru, Gopal, 63–64, 108, 115

Haavikko, Paavo, 151
Hadiya (Akhila Ashokan), 144–145
hamartia, 68
Hampi's stone chariot, 71–72
harm principle, 125
Hegel
    caste in India, 53
    critiques Oriental philosophy, 27
    equation between individual and community, 29
    individualist form of nationalism, 30
    spirit, 27
    universal (or universality), idea of, 29
Heidegger, Martin, 155
Hindi film industry/Bombay film industry, 101–102
Hindu
    cultural identity of, 80
    'good' Hindu *vs* 'bad' Hindu, 80–81, 84–86
    idea of darshan, 92–95
    other, 106
    political and ethical status of, 80–81
Hindu body, 113
Hindu-Muslim relations, 20–21, 44–49, 94–96, 177–178
    during Manto and Malihabadi's time, 97–103
    'nationalist' context of, 22
Hindu nationalism, 102
Hindu right, 84–85, 99
Hindu Sabha, 20, 22
Hindu society, 49–51, 54, 58–60, 105, 120, 122, 135
    honour killings within, 138–139

imagined political community, 1
immigrants/refugees, 73–78
    anti-foreigners movement in Assam, 74–76
    Bengali refugees in Assam, 76–77
    central problem of, 78
    Donald Trump's evocation of 'forgotten people', 77–78
Indian Muslims, 102
Indian nationalist thought, 1

Jafri, Ali Sardar, 90–94
Jahan, Shafin, 144
Jai Narain Vyas University incident, 2016, 162
Jat-Muslim riot, 2013, 145
Jayasukhlal, 46
Jeevanathan, Muthukrishnan, 117
Jinnah, Muhammad Ali, 44, 88, 178–179
justice, 65, 86–88

Kalam, A.P.J. Abdul, 85
Kalburgi, M.M., 84
Kant, Immanuel, 169, 172–174
Kar, Boddhisatva, 76
Kargil conflict, 1999, 165
Kashmir issue, 13, 69
Kaur, Gurmehar, 164–165
Khadi Pratisthan, 45
Khalid, Umar, 162
Khan, Aamir, 102
Khan, Liaquat Ali, 14
Khan, Pehlu, 134
Khan, Shahrukh, 102
Khôra, 57

Kierkegaard, Søren, 174–175
Kumar, Aishwary, 53, 108, 111–112
Kumar, Ashok, 100–101
Kumari, Ved, 163
Kurukshetra, battle of, 175–176

Lanman, Charles Rockwell, 56
Levinas, 41
love jihad, 138, 144–146
Ludhianvi, Sahir, 101

Machado, Antonio, 93
Magris, Claudio, 182
Malihabadi, Josh, 97–103
Mamdani, Mahmood, 79–80
Manto, Saadat Hasan, 97–103
Manu, 46–49
Manusmriti, 56–57, 160
Martín, Abel, 94
Marx, Karl, 66
    The German Ideology, 26–27
    history of slavery, 58–59
    property of labour, 26–27
Mayakovsky, Vladimir, 113
Mendes-Flohr, Paul, 181
Mill, James, 31
Mill, John Stuart, 31, 125
Mishra, Dipak, 128
modernity and development of modern state, 3, 18, 70–71
    in context of Ayatollah Khomeini, 72
    Nehruvian secular state, 3, 83, 86
Mukherjee, Dr Shyama Prasad, 88
Muslim League, 88
Muslims
    good and bad, 79
mythical violence, 19

Naga National Council (NNC), 14–15
Namashudras, genocide of, 5
Namboodiripad, E.M.S., 58
    caste system, 59
    The National Question in Kerala, 58–59

Nandy, Ashis, 81
    Hindu communalism, 87
Naqvi, Syed Abu Talib, 98
natural rights, 126
Nehru, Jawaharlal, 1–2, 97–98
    appropriation of Marxism, 5–6
    Autobiography, 11
    Azad Memorial Lectures, 5–6
    caste system, 4
    colonialism, 9–10
    Communist Party, 6–7
    democratic principle, 4
    The Discovery of India, 4, 6, 8, 72
    equality, 4–5
    impact of western culture on India, 9–10
    India, 12
    issue of Partition, 12–13
    Kashmir issue, 13
    modernity, 3
    Naga demand, 14–15
    non-Marxist politics, 5–6
    opposition between East and West, 8–9
    secular state, 3, 82–83, 86, 99
    social ideal, 5
    social sphere progress, 3
    spirit of man, 7–8
    spirit of the age, 8
    spiritual/material dichotomy, 8
Nellie riots, 1983, 77
Nietzsche, Friedrich, 171
Noakhali riots, 1948, 44–49, 88, 166, 173, 178

Omvedt, Gail, 58

Pansare, Govind, 84
passive resistance, 16
Paz, Octavio, 6–7, 11, 93
    One Earth, Four or Five Worlds, 72
persuasion, idea of, 168–169, 172–174, 182
poetic faith, 94, 96

political justice, 88
Poona Pact of 1932, 153
power, 151
    Gandhi's method of challenging, 152
privileged *vs* underprivileged, 65–66
public lynching, 133–134

Quit India Movement, 3

racist movements, 74
Ramjas College incident, 2017, 161–162, 164
Ranawat, Rajshree, 162
Rancière, Jacques, 26
Rao, Kiran, 102
rational conviction, 169–170
rational faith, 95–96
rationalist and modernizing nationalism, 5
Regar, Shambhulal, 137
religious nationalism, 77, 85
revivalist movements, 74
revolutionary violence, 5–6
right-wing politics, new brand of nationalism and, 102, 114–118, 161–167
Rohatgi, Mukul, 123–125
Rousseau, Jean-Jacques, 124
Roy, Dr Prafulla Chandra, 88
Rushdie, Salman, 12, 70

sanatana dharma, 17
Saramago, José, 116
Sarukkai, Sundar, 106–108
Savarkar, Veer, 81
Saxena, Ankit, 139
Saxena, Yashpal, 139
Schelling, Friedrich, 27
Schmitt, Carl, 175, 177
secular state, 82–83, 86, 99–100, 149
Seth, Sanjay, 5
Shah Bano case, 83
Sikri, A.K., 124
Singh, Maharaja Hari, 13
Singh, Mahmohan, 35
Singh, Mohinder, 24

Skaria, Ajay, 42
social contract, 124
social order, 100, 136
Socrates, 173
Suhrawardy, H.S., 45–46
Suhrud, Tridip, 64
Sukirtharani, 139
'surplus' of Indian nationalism, 1

Tagore, Rabindranath, 1, 71
    'Civilization and Progress,' 23
    critique of colonial domination, 35–36
    critique of Enlightenment rationality, 34
    critique of individual, 31–32
    culture, idea of, 23, 33
    debate with Gandhi, 24, 32, 38–40
    East-West conflict, 32–35
    human nature, culture and human consciousness, understanding of, 24–26
    individual mind, 28
    nation, understanding of, 34–35
    nationalism, idea of, 33
    nature, idea of, 28
    principle of utility, 31
    'spirit,' idea of, 33
    spiritual man, 32
    surplus man, idea of, 54
    surplus value, idea of, 25–27, 31
    universal (or universality), idea of, 24, 30, 36, 53
    Western civilization, 35–36
    'world-spirit,' idea of, 27
Tambe, Ashwini, 47
territorial morality, 69
territorial politics, 69–70, 77
Tilak, Bal Gangadhar, 16
Trump, Donald, 74, 77
trust, politics of, 12, 45, 96, 98–101, 103, 168

Universal Declaration of Human Rights, 70

universities in India, new brand of nationalism and, 161–166
The Unprecedented Defence of the Fortress Deutschkreuz (Werner Herzog), 78
untouchables/untouchability, 105–106
    distinction between Dalit and other women, 139–143
    Gandhi's untouchables as Harijan, 109–111
    hereditary untouchability, 108–109
    law of, 107
    modern form of untouchability, 55–58
    Muslims as political untouchables, 138–139, 144–149
    relationship between Hindus and untouchables, 52
    situation of tactful touchability, 107
    suicide of Dalits, 113–118
    transitory and necessary untouchability, 108, 110

Vemula, Rohith, 114–118
Venugopal, K., 128
violence, in context of anti-colonial struggle, 156–161
Vivekananda, Swami, 104
von Humboldt, Wilhelm, 175

Wacha, Suvik, 97
Wahl, Jean, 41
Weber, Max, 170
'The West,' notion of, 2

Yadoo, Adil Ahmad, 132–133